TASTING TABLE
Cooking with Friends

TASTING TABLE
Cooking with Friends

GEOFF BARTAKOVICS
and TODD COLEMAN

FLATIRON
BOOKS
NEW YORK

Recipes for
Modern
Entertaining

photography by
TODD COLEMAN

TASTING TABLE COOKING WITH FRIENDS. Copyright © 2019 by Geoff
Bartakovics. All rights reserved. Printed in the United States of America. For
information, address Flatiron Books, 175 Fifth Avenue, New York, N.Y. 10010.

Photography by Todd Coleman

www.flatironbooks.com

The Library of Congress Cataloging-in-Publication Data
is available upon request.

ISBN 978-1-250-13954-2 (paper over board)
ISBN 978-1-250-13953-5 (ebook)

Our books may be purchased in bulk for promotional, educational, or business
use. Please contact your local bookseller or the Macmillan Corporate and
Premium Sales Department at 1-800-221-7945, extension 5442, or by email at
MacmillanSpecialMarkets@macmillan.com.

FIRST EDITION: May 2019

10 9 8 7 6 5 4 3 2 1

Contents

To Jenn Hirano

TASTING TABLE
Cooking with Friends

Introduction

Tonight's party is going to be epic.

You've planned and prepped and cooked and cleaned and tablescaped your place within an inch of its life. The bar is a sparkling altar of bottles and bitters and heaping buckets of steaming ice. The candles are lit, the trash taken out. An excited calm descends as the kitchen buzzes with friends cutting lime wheels, and you suddenly wonder if you should have invited that couple from CrossFit.

You'd invite them all if there were chairs enough, you think.

The olives belong beside the gleaming glassware and you should test *just one more bite* of the Duck Fat Chex Mix ... to be certain. It's perfect. *Tonight will be perfect,* you know, even when something inevitably goes sideways.

You launch the playlist built especially for tonight, check the time as you grab a cold beer to join you in the shower. T minus 20 minutes as your better half announces, "The appetizers smell amazing!"

And you didn't martyr yourself to pull today off. A few besties arrived earlier for some cooking and catch-up ... and just enough day-drinking to keep the laughs rolling. You love these nights ... and all the thank-you texts that will arrive in the morning.

Now the sun's about to set and you notice more voices are joining the kitchen chorus. So you clock your outfit in the mirror one last time and head into the evening.

This is why I host, you're sure, *because the party is about these people and if "the medium is the message," then this fancy gathering of lowbrow friends will be shouting, "Life is good!" to anyone within earshot as the taxis pull away tonight.*

Partying together makes friendship magic in a way that seems important today, when relationships can dissolve too easily into a blur of digital "likes" from old friends we see in real life too seldom. The most effective social networking is assigned seating at a dinner, and no "activity feed" can say "I love you guys" quite the way a heartfelt toast can.

And so this book.

Todd and I have created *Tasting Table Cooking with Friends* to update the classic menu cookbook for a new generation of heroic hosts and dinner party emcees. The recipes and cocktails borrow from hot restaurant and ingredient trends to keep things cool, and we designed menus for the way we live today.

What's most modern is that each menu is designed for collaboration so that a few friends can host together. No two recipes require the oven at different temperatures at the same time, for example, and there are recipes at different skill levels so that everyone can lend a hand. Sure, you still have to manage the invitations and order the groceries. But crowdsourced cooking (and cleanup, if you're lucky) makes entertaining easier so you can do it more often.

And that's the real point of this book: We hope it will inspire you to gather more often with the people you love. To feed friendship regularly with shared experience and table-shaking laughter. To create lasting memories through meals made and enjoyed together.

To make life larger by partying harder.

So embrace your inner cruise director! Go send that save-the-date. Collide your friend groups and manage the aftermath. Borrow chairs from neighbors and build a bar with your best glasses. Top it off before you raise a toast. Lower the lights and then turn it up.

Make that party. Gather who matters. Be the magic.

—*Geoff Bartakovics, 2019*

How to Use
This Book

Cooking with Friends has been designed so that all the recipes in a menu can be prepared by a handful of cohosts cooking as a team in just a few hours. Dishes generally don't require the same tools or appliances at the same time, so you can prepare the entrée on the cooktop while one friend preps the salad near the sink and another mixes cake batter on the kitchen table.

Of course you could make these menus on your own by allowing generous lead time. Every recipe is a winner on its own or as part of a menu dreamed up entirely by you. But if you want to cook with friends the way we imagined, here are a couple of options to consider.

Option One: Team Hosting

1. **Invite a few cohosts to cook with you.** Review the recipes to decide exactly how much time you'll need for each menu, but two or three friends should be able to cook, batch the signature cocktail, and set the table in about three hours.

2. **Source the groceries, liquor, and supplies.** For a stress-free experience, have all the ingredients purchased by the night before, including basic staples (salt, sugar, butter, olive oil, not-outdated spices, foil, and plastic wrap) and equipment.

3. **Organize your kitchen and game plan.** Imagine the team layout (who's near the stove? At the sink? At the table?) and who will cook what (better cooks get harder recipes; helpful klutzes toss the salad or build the playlist). Create a station for each recipe with the required ingredients and equipment (cutting boards, knives, cookware, whisks, and kitchen towels for messes) along with a copy of the recipe. Store perishables in the fridge in a visible location so each cook can self-source their ingredients. Create a dishwashing station with hot, sudsy water and sponges and lay out a row of dry kitchen rags to create an extended drying rack so that everyone will clean as they go. Most important, set up a cute libation station with wine or beer for the team to lubricate as they cook (just watch those knives!). Avoid heavy liquor too early or the meal won't come together.

4. **Get your head in the game and cook!** Once the team has assembled, explain the plan in your least bossy, breeziest tone and get going. As the host, you should be cooking the most involved or complicated dish, since leaders lead. But also keep a helpful eye on less experienced cooks to clear up any confusion about "fine dice" and make sure no one gets stressed. The size of those chopped mushrooms won't make or break the dish, but even if it does, who cares? Laugh it off, since life is long and memories short.

Option Two:
Outsource Dishes

1. **Ask a few friends to prepare one of the dishes from the menu at home before the party.** Potlucks are generally well-intentioned but poorly executed affairs, since coordination (of dishes) and control (of quantities) are the keys to a good menu. Make like a call center and distribute the workload among several locations, working together but separately. Share the recipes (with a link to buy this book!), assigning each dish according to common sense. Vegetarians don't want to make the chicken dish— duh. And you should contribute the main dish, since you're not a cheapskate.

2. **Coordinate arrival times** with each cohost, depending on whether their dish will need to be cooked at your place or just "finished" (reheated or plated for prettiness). That way all the recipes will be ready at the same time.

3. **When the feasting is over, set up a dishwashing station** so cohosts can return home with a clean dish, and don't forget to have plenty of to-go containers ready to send leftovers home with their makers.

Pro-Tip

Order as many supplies and ingredients as possible, well in advance. Nearly every liquor or wine store will take a decent-sized order by phone and deliver it to your home. **Home goods are easily acquired online** at the best prices, so order those napkins, extra aprons, and (lightly) scented candles early. But, yes, you still need to stop by the gas station or deli for forty pounds of ice a couple of hours before party time.

About the Cocktails

Nothing says "I'm a grown up" like a properly mixed drink to launch the night. To keep the vibe current, our cocktails generally update classics with unexpected base spirits or recent ingredient obsessions—like a gimlet made with tequila instead of gin and garnished with basil rather than a lime twist.

Each boozy beverage is designed for "batching," which is bartender-speak for "make it before the guests arrive." Always combine the nonalcoholic components in a large beaker or pitcher, which you will keep on ice (not with ice in it, to prevent dilution). Set the nonalcoholic component at the bar beside the spirit, a few measuring jiggers, and a simple recipe card in clear block letters that explains the recipe in shorthand that even a novice drinker will understand. Like, "1 jigger JUICE + 2 jiggers TEQUILA → shake with ICE → strain + BASIL." Assign an early arriver to play bartender at the start to show guests the way.

Sangria and Snacks

MENU

There was a time long ago when everyone in your life had so much free time that you'd spend endless hours around town talking about nothing with anyone for no reason in particular. Over coffee or a snack, friendships were formed, futures planned, and memories made.

But today, it feels impossible to gather your tribe for anything less major than a wedding. An invitation to a party at your place better hit inboxes a least a month in advance if you hope for more than half your friends to still be available on the night in question. Sigh.

Here's a tip to fight *early-onset boring* as you adultify: Avoid prime-time calendar competition by inviting friends for light snacks and a catch-up on a weekend afternoon instead.

Guests won't expect a spread at that hour, but it'll be hard to say no to spicy deviled eggs and gyro meatballs when they're merchandised so effortlessly around your living room. Offer a thought-provoking green pepper sangria, serve a bit of hot goss, and your guests might end up late for their "can't miss" dinner plans.

If you do it right, folks will complain that they "wish we could do this more often." In fact you can, you'll tell them: You're launching a monthly book club (or wine club or other regular ruse) at the same time and place and can't wait to see them again soon. This menu will work great for that, too.

Skill Level

Put your best cooks on the tart and blondies; those dishes require a bit more kitchen dexterity.

Special Equipment

- Punch bowl

- Pastry bag with tip

- Bamboo cocktail skewers

- Two 18 x 13-inch rimmed sheet pans

Game Plan

- **The Day Before:** Freeze the ice mold for the sangria (if using)

- **Three Hours Before:** Make the eggplant

- **Two Hours Before:** Make the blondies and tart

- **One Hour Before:** Make the eggs and meatballs and finish the sangria

- **30 Minutes Before:** Make the dates

Wine Ideas

A hearty Italian rosé with more color than usual is perfect for this afternoon menu: The stronger fruit will lend texture to the rosé. (For wine newbies, "textured" means "bold enough to compete with roasted meats like gyro meatballs.")

Regarding drinks: It's better to have extra for your next party than to run out.

Pro-Tip:
The "0-1-2" Rule

For a light-snacks get-together like this one, remember this: When there will be **zero** tables, serve items that can be held easily using **one** hand and eaten in **two** bites, max. Small appetizers, crudités, and chips can be enjoyed while moving around the party—without needing to balance a plate and a fork on a glass or a napkin.

Party Math:
How Much Wine and Beer?

If you're offering a welcome cocktail, guests will drink less wine and beer, but it's better to have extra for your next party than to run out.

- **Wine:** ½ bottle per guest per hour

- **Beer:** 2 bottles or cans per person per hour

Fruity sangrias can be delicious, but let's face it, they're not going to win you any points in the originality category. The green pepper in this sangria is just weird enough to surprise and delight ("A *vegetable sangria?* Well, *I've never!"*). If you decide to go the classic punch bowl route, make a single large ice mold by freezing water and slices of green apple and lemon in a bowl overnight.

GREEN PEPPER SANGRIA

MAKES 16 to 20 cocktails
SKILL LEVEL 1

3 bottles Grüner Veltliner (or any dry white wine)

¾ cup Lillet Blanc

3 green apples, thinly sliced into rounds

1 green bell pepper, seeded and thinly sliced into rings

3 lemons, cut into wheels

2 limes, cut into wheels

In large pitchers or a punch bowl, combine all the ingredients. Allow to sit for at least 1 hour to allow the flavors to come together. Chill with a large ice mold (see headnote) or serve over ice cubes.

Deviled eggs are usually a crowd-pleaser, and sriracha has been having a moment for so long it's becoming the new ketchup. Bring them together in these spicy deviled eggs for a surefire hit. To add a creamy, subtle tanginess, substitute yogurt for the mayonaise. And if filling the whites with a pastry bag or snipped zip-top bag seems too fussy, just plop that filling in with a spoon and be done; they'll be enjoyed just the same.

SERVES 8 to 10
SKILL LEVEL 2

SPICY DEVILED EGGS

12 large eggs

½ cup mayonnaise

2 tablespoons sriracha or a similar hot chili paste

Pickled red chiles or Peppadews, sliced (optional)

Cilantro leaves (optional)

Maldon salt (optional)

1

Place the eggs in a large pot and cover with cold water by 2 inches. Bring to a boil, cover, and remove from the heat. Let sit for 8 minutes. Drain. Peel the eggs under cold running water.

2

Cut the eggs in half lengthwise. Remove the yolks and place in a medium bowl. Put the whites on a serving platter. If you want to be fancy, slice off a bit of the bottom of each white so that they will sit flat on the platter.

3

Mash the egg yolks with a fork and add the mayo and sriracha. Mix well with a fork. Spoon the mixture into a zip-top bag, then snip off a bottom corner and pipe the mixture into the egg white halves. Chill until you're ready to eat. Right before you serve, garnish each with chiles, cilantro leaves, and a sprinkle of Maldon salt, if desired.

This recipe makes that diner favorite, lamb gyros, into party-portable meatballs, with both hot and white sauces to dress them up. Not into balls or a smoky kitchen? Just flatten them into mini patties and give the gyro meat a sear on your charcoal grill instead.

GYRO MEATBALLS WITH HOT SAUCE, WHITE SAUCE

FOR THE MEATBALLS

2 pounds ground lamb

1 small onion, finely chopped

3 garlic cloves, finely chopped

1 tablespoon fresh oregano leaves, minced

2 teaspoons kosher salt

1 teaspoon sweet paprika

1 teaspoon ground cumin

1 teaspoon ground black pepper

¾ teaspoon dried mint

½ teaspoon fresh thyme leaves

¼ teaspoon ground nutmeg

¼ cup olive oil

FOR THE WHITE SAUCE

1 cup mayonnaise

¼ cup sour cream

2 teaspoons white wine vinegar

½ teaspoon dried dill

Kosher salt and freshly ground black pepper

Sriracha

1

MAKE THE MEATBALLS: In a large bowl, mix together all the meatball ingredients except for the oil. Using your hands, form the mixture into 50 to 60 (1-inch) balls. Transfer the meatballs to a baking sheet and refrigerate until firm, about 30 minutes.

2

MEANWHILE, MAKE THE WHITE SAUCE: In a medium bowl, mix together all the sauce ingredients, except sriracha, plus ¼ cup water. Taste and season with salt and pepper. Refrigerate until ready to serve.

3

Heat the oil in a nonstick skillet over medium-high heat. Working in batches, cook the meatballs, turning occasionally, until browned but still pink in the center (160°F by USDA recommendation), about 6 minutes per batch. Arrange the meatballs on a platter or in paper cones and place a cocktail skewer in each. Serve with bowls of white sauce and sriracha.

Puff pastry is an entertainer's secret weapon: easy to use (just thaw and bake), great looking (all those layers!), and infinitely adaptable (just about anything can go on top). Once you've mastered this easy tart, swap in other cheeses, like Gorgonzola or goat cheese, or top with entirely different meats and veggies, like prosciutto or olives and onions.

SERVES 8 to 10
SKILL LEVEL 4

TOMATO TART WITH FETA AND ZA'ATAR

1 sheet frozen puff pastry, thawed and kept chilled, rolled into a 10 × 13–inch rectangle

2 shallots, finely chopped

1 pint grape or cherry tomatoes, halved

5 ounces feta cheese, crumbled (about 1 cup)

2 tablespoons za'atar seasoning, plus more for serving

¼ cup extra-virgin olive oil

1
Preheat the oven to 350°F. Line an 18 × 13–inch sheet pan with parchment paper.

2
Fit the pastry into the prepared pan, pressing the excess pastry against the sides of the pan. With a paring knife, score around bottom inner edge of the pastry (just inside the crease where the bottom meets the sides), being careful not to cut all the way through. Prick the bottom of the pastry all over with a fork, line with a sheet of parchment paper that covers the bottom only, and fill with dried beans or pie weights. Bake until the edge of the crust begins to puff and color, about 25 minutes. Remove the beans and paper. Bake until the bottom is golden, 6 to 8 minutes more. Let the crust cool.

3
Sprinkle the bottom of the cooled pastry with the shallots and tomatoes, cover evenly with the feta, then sprinkle with the za'atar. Bake for 15 minutes.

4
Drizzle the top of the tart with the oil. Bake until the crust is deep golden, about 10 minutes more. Let cool to room temperature.

5
To serve, sprinkle the tart with another tablespoon or so of za'atar and cut into squares.

2 large eggplants

1 medium yellow onion, sliced

2 garlic cloves

¼ cup extra-virgin olive oil

½ cup full-fat Greek yogurt

¼ cup walnuts, toasted and roughly chopped

¼ cup loosely packed fresh mint, torn, plus more for garnish

Kosher salt, to taste

1 tablespoon pomegranate molasses

Pomegranate seeds (optional)

Aleppo pepper (optional)

Pita chips, for serving

"Plating" is pretentious shorthand for "helping an ugly dish feel pretty." This delicious eggplant dip didn't win the genetics lottery when it was born a meh color and gloppy texture, but you can dress it up nicely by serving it in a colorful, oversized dish, sprinkling it with additional mint and pomegranate seeds, and artistically drizzling ruby pomegranate molasses syrup over the dish like Jackson Pollock.

SMOKY EGGPLANT WITH YOGURT, MINT, AND TOASTED WALNUTS

1

Preheat the oven to 450°F.

2

Put the whole eggplants, onion, garlic, and olive oil on a sheet pan and toss. Prick the eggplants with a sharp knife a few times. Roast until the eggplants have collapsed and are blackened in spots and the onion is dark and tender, about 45 minutes. Let cool slightly.

3

Split open the eggplants. Scoop out the flesh and place in a colander for 10 minutes to drain off any excess liquid; discard the stems and skin.

4

Put the drained cooled eggplant flesh, roasted onion and garlic, yogurt, most of the walnuts, the mint, and the salt into a food processor. Process until just smooth. Taste and season with salt.

5

Using a rubber spatula, spread the eggplant mixture in a shallow bowl. Drizzle with the pomegranate molasses and sprinkle with the reserved walnuts, additional mint, and pomegranate seeds and Aleppo pepper, if desired. Serve with pita chips.

Just about anything savory stuffed into a date makes a great last-minute party nibble. These are even more delicious after a trip to a very hot oven and a cool-down shower in refreshing lemon juice. Prepare them in advance but don't cook them until your guests are due to arrive, since they're best when piping hot.

SERVES 8 to 10
SKILL LEVEL 1

BACON-WRAPPED WALNUT-AND-GOAT-CHEESE-STUFFED DATES

1 cup crumbled goat cheese, at room temperature

½ cup walnuts, toasted

2 tablespoons extra-virgin olive oil

1½ teaspoons kosher salt

1½ teaspoons coarsely ground black pepper

24 dates (preferably Deglet Noor), pitted

1 pound thin bacon, cut crosswise in half

1 lemon, cut into wedges, for serving

1

Preheat the oven to 450°F. Line a sheet pan with aluminum foil.

2

Put the goat cheese, walnuts, olive oil, salt, and pepper in a food processor and blend until smooth. Spoon the filling into a pastry bag (or zip-top bag with a small corner snipped off). Squeeze the goat cheese mixture into the cavity of each date.

3

Tightly wrap each date with half a slice of bacon and place, seam-side down, on the prepared sheet pan. About 30 minutes before you're ready to serve, put the pan in the oven and bake for 20 minutes, until the dates are sizzling and the bacon is crisp. Let cool for a few minutes, then serve with a squeeze of lemon.

Blondies are those coffee-counter staples who think they're brownies' clever cousins. They've never really done it for us, with their one-note sweetness and air of superiority. But this recipe upgrades the typical blondie by adding tahini and sea salt to provide the depth and complexity that their character has lacked. You'll gain some brawn to match blondie's new brains as you struggle to combine the chocolate chips into that thick batter. Keep swirling: This recipe is worth the arm workout.

SERVES 8 to 10
SKILL LEVEL 3

½ cup (1 stick) unsalted butter, plus more for greasing the pan

2 cups all-purpose flour, plus more for preparing the pan

1½ cups light brown sugar

½ cup well-stirred tahini

2 large eggs, beaten

1 teaspoon vanilla extract

1½ teaspoons baking powder

¼ teaspoon fine sea salt

¾ cup semisweet chocolate chips

2 teaspoons sesame seeds

Maldon salt

TAHINI CHOCOLATE BLONDIES

1

Preheat the oven to 350°F. Butter and flour an 18 × 13–inch sheet pan.

2

Melt the butter. In a large bowl, mix together the butter, brown sugar, and tahini and let cool to room temperature. Beat in the eggs and vanilla.

3

In a medium bowl, whisk together the flour, baking powder, and fine sea salt. Add the dry ingredients to the wet ingredients and mix just until a smooth batter is formed. Add ¼ cup of the chocolate chips and sesame seeds to the batter and stir to combine. Transfer the batter to the prepared pan. Sprinkle the remaining ½ cup chocolate chips on top.

4

Bake for 3 minutes and remove from the oven. Using a butter knife, swirl the chocolate chips into the batter (this will be difficult, as the batter will have started to set). Sprinkle a pinch or two of Maldon salt on top. Return the pan to the oven and bake until lightly browned and toothpick inserted into the center comes out clean, about 20 minutes. Cool for 15 minutes before cutting the blondies into 12 squares, then cutting each in half into triangles.

Heavy Apps Before a Big Night Out

MENU

Your friend-family deserves a big night out—the kind that begins with extensive outfit changes, dances its way through several clubs and house parties, and ends circa sunrise with new friends you just met on the other side of town. These are the legendary nights of unplanned high jinks, beer-goggle romance, and stolen leather jackets that you'll reminisce about for years afterward.

Be a hosting hero by inviting your funnest friends for "pregame" appetizers at your place a couple of hours before the club. Folks will nibble and sip excitedly until the latecomers finally trickle in (pomade is tricky! they insist). Suddenly it's late enough to head out into the night, moving this pumped-up crew out of your still-neat home before anyone has a chance to dump a bottle of red on the new sofa.

The hors d'oeuvres in this menu are substantial enough to fill guests up with food before they drink too much about town, like ranch-crusted baby back ribs and pepperoncini that ooze with goat cheese and salmon. The pregame cocktail is a sophisticated Boulevardier Spritz for a bright roll into the dark night. And, best of all, dessert is a Patrón XO espresso milkshake roadie, since no one is driving. Champion.

Then it's time to go lose your phone, keys, and/or dignity. But don't worry: We've got you on our prayer list.

Skill Level

Your most skilled guest will make quick work of the ribs. Let your more most meticulous friend tackle the the nachos, since symmetry and even topping are keys to that dish's success. Anyone can lend a hand with the pepperoncini.

Special Equipment

- Punch bowl

- 12-inch cast-iron skillet

- Three 18 x 13–inch rimmed sheet pans

Game Plan

- **The Night Before:** Make the pretzel mix

- **Three Hours Before:** Make the ribs

- **Two Hours Before:** Make the dip

- **One Hour Before:** Make the pepperoncini

- **45 Minutes Before:** Make the nachos

- **Right Before Serving:** Make the spritz

- **As Things Are Wrapping Up:** Make the milkshakes

Be a hosting hero by inviting your funnest friends for "pregame" appetizers at your place a couple of hours before the club.

It's time to go lose your phone, keys, and/or your dignity.

Wine Ideas

Serious dishes that pair well with a crisp white wine deserve an Alsace Pinot Blanc. It's simple but textured and usually has a touch of fruit that's great with smoked fish like salmon. Try a hearty spiced Loire Valley Cabernet Franc with the ranchy ribs and the chorizo.

Pro-Tip:
All Good Things Must End

Always include an end time on your invitations (a three-hour cocktail party or four-hour dinner are typical), even for a loose affair. You can always extend if you like, but humans need a sense of urgency to inspire action. Folks will show on time if they know the fun won't last forever, whereas an invitation that says "until late" suggests that guests can show when they like. That's a recipe for a listless gathering, and a half-empty party is like a sad clown: all dressed up but missing the point.

Spritzes are usually light, but ours packs a punch, so serve up small pours. If budget allows, we like Carpano Antica Formula, a classy Italian sweet vermouth with strong vanilla notes. And that leftover Antica is also your backup plan if the Spritz runs low: just serve it straight over ice with an orange wheel garnish like the classic aperitif that it is.

BOULEVARDIER SPRITZ

MAKES 18 to 20 punch-size cocktails

SKILL LEVEL 1

2 cups bourbon

2 cups Campari

2 cups Carpano Antica Formula sweet vermouth (any sweet vermouth will do but this is the best)

1 (750-milliliter) bottle dry cider

3 navel oranges, for garnish

1

In a large punch bowl or pitcher, combine the bourbon, Campari, vermouth, and cider. If making ahead, don't add the cider until just before serving so the drink won't lose its fizz.

2

Cut large strips of zest from 1 orange using a vegetable peeler to add to the bowl, and cut small twists from the other 2 oranges to serve on the side as individual garnishes. Serve over ice.

We googled the heck out of it, but we can't seem to find a non-German word to describe the emotion evoked when the cocktail nut mix is so addictive that you want to unload the whole bowl into your grubby palm and inhale the salty payload like air itself. It's part furtive delight, part shame (you should share, you pig!) and all savory desire. For lack of a term, we're calling it "Salty-Sweetish Pretzel and Nut Mix." Make it the night before your party, since you'll need all your sheet pans for the other recipes. And don't forget to line those pans with parchment or foil for easy cleanup.

SERVES 8 to 10
SKILL LEVEL 2

SALTY-SWEETISH PRETZEL AND NUT MIX

2 cups small pretzels

1½ cups sesame sticks

1½ cups raw pecans

1 cup raw cashews

1 cup raw walnuts

½ cup packed light brown sugar

1 tablespoon very finely chopped fresh rosemary

2 tablespoons Madras curry powder

1 tablespoon kosher salt

1½ teaspoons coarsely ground black pepper

½ cup (1 stick) unsalted butter

2 cups unsweetened coconut chips

Maldon salt

1 cup dried sour cherries

1
Position racks in the upper and lower thirds of the oven and preheat the oven to 350°F. Line two sheet pans with parchment paper.

2
Combine the pretzels, sesame sticks, pecans, cashews, and walnuts in a medium bowl. Set aside.

3
In a large bowl, stir together the brown sugar, rosemary, curry powder, kosher salt, and pepper.

4
In a small skillet over medium heat, melt the butter. Cook, swirling the pan occasionally, until the butter lightly browns and smells nutty, about 4 minutes. Immediately pour the melted butter into the bowl with the spice mixture and stir to coat. Add the pretzel-nut mixture and fold gently until every piece is well coated.

5
Divide the mixture between the prepared sheet pans and spread it into one even

RECIPE CONTINUES

layer. Bake for 15 minutes. Divide the coconut chips evenly between the sheet pans and stir well to combine. Clumping is good! You want things to stick together—to make yummy clusters. Return the pans to the oven, swapping their positions, and bake, without stirring, until the nuts and coconut are lightly toasted, 15 to 20 minutes more. Remove from the oven, immediately sprinkle lightly with Maldon salt to taste, and let cool completely. (To encourage clumping, do not disturb the nut mix as it is cooling.)

6

When cool, add the dried cherries, gently toss to combine, transfer to small bowls, and serve.

5 Excuses
to Host a Party

The best reason to host a party is no reason at all. But if you need to convince yourself (or your partner or roommates), consider these excuses . . . er . . . occasions:

1. To celebrate a friend's recently released book, album, app, or child (from the womb)

2. To convert loose acquaintanceships with cool-seeming folks from work/CrossFit/ playgroup into actual friendships

3. To show off the wedding gifts you'll use only once before packing them into the basement or selling them on eBay

4. To source a new mate after a devastating breakup: Ask each guest to (1) bring a single friend you might be into; and (2) post at least one Insta of you looking great so your ex will see . . .

5. To reduce your spirits/ wine/beer inventory before moving or detoxing

Even friends who don't think they love ranch dressing will fall for these ribs. This recipe's genius involves using homemade magic ranch dust twice, first as a rub for the ribs, then as the flavoring in a crème fraîche dipping sauce. You may want to double the recipe to ensure leftover dust, which you can dole out to your guests in baggies as a topping for the popcorn that will accompany their hangover movie marathon.

SERVES 8 to 10
SKILL LEVEL 3

RANCH-CRUSTED BABY BACK RIBS WITH BUTTERMILK RANCH DIPPING SAUCE

¼ cup onion powder

¼ cup garlic powder

2 tablespoons kosher salt

2 tablespoons light brown sugar

2 tablespoons dried chives

2 tablespoons dried parsley

2 tablespoons dried dill

4 teaspoons freshly ground black pepper

3 (3-pound) racks baby back ribs

1½ cups full-fat buttermilk

2 (4-ounce) containers crème fraîche

1

Preheat the oven to 325°F. Line two sheet pans with wire racks.

2

In a small bowl, whisk together the onion powder, garlic powder, salt, brown sugar, chives, parsley, dill, and pepper. Reserve 2 tablespoons of the spice mixture for sprinkling on the finished ribs.

3

Rub each rack of ribs with about ¼ cup of the spice mixture, then place two racks on one prepared sheet pan and the third rack on the other pan. Cover each pan tightly with aluminum foil and roast, rotating the pans halfway through, until the ribs are tender when pierced with a knife, about 2 hours.

4

Meanwhile, add the buttermilk and crème fraîche to the small bowl with the remaining spice mixture and whisk together into a smooth dressing. Refrigerate until ready to use.

RECIPE CONTINUES

5

Once the ribs are tender, remove the pans from the oven and raise the oven temperature to 450°F. Discard the foil and brush each rack of ribs with 3 tablespoons of the ranch dressing. Return the pans to the oven and roast, rotating the pans halfway through, until golden, 20 to 25 minutes.

6

Transfer the ribs to a cutting board and let rest for 5 minutes, then cut into individual ribs. Sprinkle the ribs with the reserved 2 tablespoons spice mixture. Serve the ribs on a platter drizzled with some of the ranch dressing and with the remainder of the dressing in a bowl on the side.

Cook the components of this dish in any order you like, but wait to assemble and bake the nachos until just before your guests arrive. Social psychology tell us that people are attracted to those who are slightly better variations of people they know. These relatable sheet pan nachos will make your guests fall instantly in love with the comfort foods they recognize, all dressed up with chorizo and roasted corn. The night is yours for the taking, nachos.

"HALF AND HALF" CHORIZO AND ROASTED CORN SHEET PAN NACHOS

FOR THE PICO DE GALLO

1 pound vine-ripe tomatoes (4 medium), cored and diced

2 tablespoons olive oil

1 teaspoon finely grated lime zest

2 tablespoons fresh lime juice

2 tablespoons minced fresh cilantro

2 garlic cloves, finely grated

½ red onion, diced

½ serrano chile, stemmed, seeded, and minced

Kosher salt and freshly ground black pepper

FOR THE ROASTED CORN

3 cups corn kernels (from 4 cobs)

¼ cup olive oil

1 teaspoon smoked paprika

¼ teaspoon cayenne pepper

Kosher salt and freshly ground black pepper

FOR THE CHORIZO

1 tablespoon olive oil

8 ounces fresh chorizo, casing removed

1

MAKE THE PICO DE GALLO: In a medium bowl, toss all the pico de gallo ingredients to combine. Set aside while you prepare the nachos.

2

MAKE THE ROASTED CORN: Preheat the broiler. On a sheet pan, toss all the roasted corn ingredients together to coat. Broil until golden and lightly charred, 4 to 5 minutes. Set aside. Set the oven to 450°F.

3

COOK THE CHORIZO: In a medium skillet, heat the olive oil over medium-high heat. Add the chorizo and cook, using a wooden spoon to break it up, until golden brown, about 5 minutes. Set aside.

4

MAKE THE GUACAMOLE: Combine all the guacamole ingredients in a medium bowl and mash with a fork until chunky. Set aside.

5

ASSEMBLE THE NACHOS: On a sheet pan, lay out half the bag of tortilla chips. On half the pan, sprinkle a quarter of

INGREDIENTS CONTINUE

RECIPE CONTINUES

FOR THE GUACAMOLE

2 avocados, halved, pitted, and peeled

2 tablespoons pickled jalapeño brine (from a jar or can of pickled jalapenõs)

1 tablespoon fresh lime juice

Kosher salt

TO ASSEMBLE

1 (13-ounce) bag tortilla chips

1 (15-ounce) can black beans, drained and rinsed

2 cups (8-ounce bag) shredded Monterey Jack cheese

Pickled jalapeño slices

Sour cream

Crumbled cotija cheese

Lime wedges

the roasted corn, and on the other half, sprinkle half the chorizo. Scatter half the black beans on the chorizo side and half the cheese over the entire pan, then repeat this layering process with the remaining tortilla chips, another quarter of the corn, and the remaining chorizo, beans, and cheese. Bake until the cheese has melted and the chips are crisp, 8 to 10 minutes.

6

Spoon the pico de gallo and guacamole over the chorizo half of the nachos, then garnish with pickled jalapeño slices. On the corn side of the nachos, scatter the remaining corn, then dollop sour cream on top and garnish with crumbled cotija cheese. Serve immediately with lime wedges alongside.

Hate salmon? Pepperoncini are easy-breezy about whom you bring to the party, so swap in diced salami or ham instead.

SERVES 8 to 10
SKILL LEVEL 1

GOAT CHEESE-STUFFED PEPPERONCINI

4 ounces soft goat cheese, at room temperature

3 ounces smoked salmon, finely chopped

2 (12-ounce) jars large whole pepperoncini, drained and patted dry

Poppy seeds, optional

Smoked paprika, optional

1

In a small bowl, combine the goat cheese and smoked salmon.

2

Lay the pepperoncini flat on a cutting board and make a long lengthwise slit on each pepper. Fill each with 2 to 3 teaspoons of the goat cheese mixture. Top with poppy seeds and paprika, if desired, and serve.

1 teaspoon cumin seeds

1 teaspoon coriander seeds

2 tablespoons olive oil

12 ounces shishito peppers, stemmed

Kosher salt

¾ teaspoon smoked paprika

⅓ cup sour cream

Zest and juice of 1 lime

1 small garlic clove, finely grated

Mixed raw veggies, such as Persian cucumbers, small peeled carrots, radishes, and cauliflower, for serving

This is one of those surprising dishes where the finished product tastes so much better than its simple ingredients . . . thanks to some strong heat and that heavy-as-hell cast-iron pan you say you love but rarely use. First the cast iron transforms cumin and coriander seeds from flat to fragrant with a quick stroke of heat, then it easily chars the peppers into blistery glory. Don't bother removing the seeds from the peppers—they're rarely spicy, and if the rare one is, you'll enjoy the minor jolt.

SMOKY SHISHITO DIP WITH RAW VEGGIES

1

Heat a 12-inch cast-iron skillet over medium-high heat. Add the cumin and coriander seeds to the skillet and toast, shaking the pan, until fragrant, 1 to 2 minutes. Transfer to a spice grinder or mortar and pestle and grind until fine. Set aside.

2

Increase the heat under the skillet to high. When it begins to smoke, add the olive oil and swirl to coat. Add the shishitos and season generously with salt, shaking the pan to distribute evenly. Cook, stirring occasionally, until the shishitos are well charred and cooked through, about 7 minutes. Add the paprika and ground spices and continue to cook until fragrant, about 30 seconds more. Scrape the contents of the skillet onto a plate and let cool.

3

In a food processor, combine the sour cream, lime zest and juice, garlic, shishitos, and any accumulated juices from the plate. Process until smooth and season to taste with salt. Transfer to a serving vessel and chill until ready to serve, at least 1 hour. Serve with veggies for dipping.

Your "heavy apps" cocktail party made reference to all the elements of a proper dinner, so it would be a miss to skip dessert. Just when guests start calling the car services to take your party deep into the night, whip up these milkshakes, top with a small floater (don't get your guests trashed too early, though!), and serve in paper to-go cups with straws (lipstick wearers will appreciate the thoughtfulness).

SERVES 8 to 10
SKILL LEVEL 1

BOOZY TO-GO ESPRESSO MILKSHAKES

2 pints vanilla ice cream

½ cup Patrón XO Café liqueur (or other coffee liqueur), chilled, plus more for floaters if you're feeling buzzy

Maldon sea salt, chocolate shavings, or a half-and-half mixture of instant espresso powder and sugar, for topping

1

If the ice cream is very hard, remove it from freezer and let sit on the counter to soften slightly, about 10 minutes. In a pinch, nuke it in 10-second increments until soft enough.

2

In a blender, combine the ice cream and Patrón. Blend until smooth, in batches if necessary, and transfer to eight glasses or to-go cups. Top with Maldon salt, chocolate, or espresso powder–sugar mixture. Drink and go!

A Make-and-Take Picnic

MENU

Picnics can evoke preciousness, with their reputations for fancy wicker baskets and camera-ready lawn blankets (see our photo on pages 72–73!). We're suckers for a stunning Instagram overhead, but today we're not shooting for picture-perfect enjoyment, and pretense is not on the menu. That blue IKEA bag will do just fine, thank you.

Maybe let's not even call this a picnic. It's a "choose-your-own-adventure meal" that lets you make the menu as you will to take wherever you like. With room-temp-friendly dishes and Tupperware confidence, our "picnic" is ready for camping or glamping or simply escaping (your apartment? your life?) for just one meal.

Choose to serve the pan bagnat sandwiches on a bright Sunday sail . . . or out the back of your boyfriend's Bronco as a post-concert tailgate. Pass the pasta salad across a plush lawn at "opera in the park" or pour the sangria from a thermos on a tarred rooftop in the middle of the steaming city.

Make and take, then eat and drink, this simple menu with some worthy friends anywhere—except where you are right now.

Skill Level

Put your strongest kitchen help on the shortbread bars—the rest of the dishes are a breeze for beginners.

Special Equipment

- 9-inch square baking pan

- 18 x 13-inch rimmed sheet pan

Game Plan

- **The Night Before:** Make the pan bagnat

- **Three Hours Before:** Make the shortbread bars

- **Two Hours Before:** Make the strawberries

- **One Hour Before:** Make the pasta and snow peas

- **45 Minutes Before:** Make the sangria

Make and take, then eat and drink, this simple menu with some worthy friends anywhere—except where you are right now.

We developed this sangria so you can pour the finished product back into the original container to create an "adult juice box." It's easy to transport without spills to your picnic location and the boxy shape will sorta conceal your buzzy intention from the forest ranger. Win-win.

MAKES 12 to 16 drinks
SKILL LEVEL 1

BOXED WINE SANGRIA

2 (1-liter) boxes light red wine with pour spouts

1 cup thinly sliced strawberries

1 cup thinly sliced lemon

½ cup peach nectar

½ cup fresh lemon juice

1 cup Grand Marnier

1

Open the boxes of wine and empty about a quarter of each into a quart container to drink separately.

2

Divide the strawberries, lemons, peach nectar, lemon juice, and Grand Marnier evenly between the boxes. Screw the tops back on the boxes and shake to combine the ingredients.

3

Refrigerate for 30 minutes to 1 hour to chill and let the ingredients steep.

4

Serve over ice.

You can probably tell by now that we're on a pickling kick at Tasting Table. Don't get over the trend until you try these strawberries, though. If you're feeling traditional, serve with crackers or baguette instead of endive leaves.

SERVES 6 to 8
SKILL LEVEL 2

PICKLED STRAWBERRIES WITH FRESH RICOTTA AND HONEY

½ cup red wine vinegar

¼ cup sugar

1½ teaspoons kosher salt

1½ pounds strawberries, hulled and quartered

8 ounces fresh ricotta

6 Belgian endives, core ends trimmed, leaves separated

Honey, for drizzling

Freshly ground black pepper, for garnish

1

In a small pot, combine the red wine vinegar, sugar, and salt and bring to a boil. Put the strawberries in a heatproof medium bowl. Pour the pickling liquid over the strawberries and let cool to room temperature. Cover and chill until ready to serve.

2

Serve the pickled strawberries with fresh ricotta and endive leaves. Drizzle with honey for added sweetness and garnish with a sprinkle of black pepper.

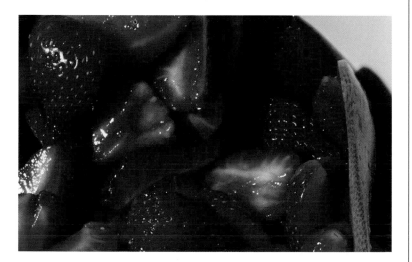

4 large eggs

½ cup pitted oil-cured black olives

4 anchovy fillets, packed in oil

1 garlic clove, smashed

2 teaspoons fresh thyme leaves

¼ cup plus 2 tablespoons olive oil

2 tablespoons Dijon mustard

2 tablespoons red wine vinegar

Kosher salt and freshly ground black pepper

12 ounces water-packed canned tuna, drained

2 (5 × 12-inch) semolina loaves, or 1 large ciabatta loaf

3 tablespoons harissa

8 ounces heirloom tomatoes, sliced

1 small red onion, thinly sliced

2 Persian cucumbers, thinly sliced, or 1 regular cucumber, peeled and thinly sliced

½ cup sliced pepperoncini

This big beauty is unruly until you weigh it down. After the 30 minutes to 8 hours in the fridge, the sandwich will be compact and the flavors concentrated.

PAN BAGNAT WITH TUNA, HARISSA, AND OLIVE TAPENADE

1

Place the eggs in a single layer in a saucepan just large enough to accommodate them. Fill the saucepan with enough cold water to cover the eggs by at least an inch. Bring the water to a boil over high heat, then remove the pot from the heat, cover, and set a timer for 7 minutes. After 7 minutes, uncover, pour out the hot water from the pot, and fill the pot with cold water and ice. Let stand for 1 minute, then remove the eggs from the water, crack them, and return them to the ice water. Let stand until completely cool, then drain the boiled eggs and carefully peel. Once peeled, rinse the eggs under cold running water to remove any remaining bits of shell. Slice the eggs lengthwise ¼ inch thick.

2

In a food processor, combine the olives, anchovies, garlic, thyme, ¼ cup of the olive oil, 1 tablespoon of the Dijon mustard, 1 tablespoon of the vinegar, ½ teaspoon salt, and a few grinds of pepper. Pulse until smooth. Season the tapenade to taste with salt and pepper.

3

In a small bowl, combine the tuna and the remaining 2 tablespoons olive oil, 1 tablespoon Dijon mustard, and 1 tablespoon vinegar. Season with salt and pepper.

4

To build the sandwich, slice open the loaves. Slather the top halves with the olive tapenade and the bottom

RECIPE CONTINUES

halves with the harissa. Top the bottom halves evenly with the sliced eggs and season with salt and pepper. Top with the tomatoes, red onion, and cucumbers. Season with salt and pepper. Top with the tuna mixture and pepperoncini.

5

Close the sandwiches and wrap them in aluminum foil. Place a baking sheet on top of the sandwiches and weigh it down with a heavy skillet and/or some heavy cans. Transfer the weighted sandwiches to the refrigerator to rest for at least 30 minutes or up to 8 hours.

6

Before serving, remove the foil and cut each sandwich into 12 small individual sandwiches.

Pack That Picnic

- Picnic baskets are made for Instagram, but an unbustable bag with shoulder-length handles will actually hold all this stuff without adding weight.

- Next-gen melamine plates come in beautiful patterns, and modern acrylic cups are so clear they look like glass.

- Don't forget several large garbage bags for collecting trash and containing dirty dishes for the return trip.

- Place temperature-sensitive dishes in freezer bags with one of those ice packs you've been collecting in your freezer.

- Usually forgotten: a few large serving utensils, napkins, Wet-Naps, full-charged Bluetooth speaker, sunscreen.

- Canned beer is much lighter than bottled, and many lightweight boxed wines aren't gross. Don't forget a few water bottles, too.

We like the sophisticated look of campanelle or gigli pasta, but really any elbow or other short-cut noodles will work here. The addition of chickpeas adds a nice protein profile to the dish to satisfy your athletic friends. They also taste great.

SERVES 6 to 8
SKILL LEVEL 2

MEDITERRANEAN CHICKPEA PASTA SALAD

2 pints cherry tomatoes

1 bulb fennel, core removed, chopped

4 tablespoons olive oil

Kosher salt and freshly ground black pepper

8 ounces dried campanelle or gigli pasta

4 ounces crème fraîche (½ cup)

Zest and juice of 1 lemon

¼ cup lightly packed fresh mint, chopped

¼ cup lightly packed fresh basil, chopped

1 (15-ounce) can chickpeas, drained and rinsed

1

Preheat the oven to 450°F. On an 18 x 13–inch rimmed sheet pan, toss the tomatoes and fennel with 2 tablespoons of the olive oil and season with salt and pepper. Roast until the tomatoes have burst and the fennel is tender, 15 to 20 minutes.

2

Meanwhile, bring a large pot of salted water to a boil. Cook the pasta until al dente according to the package instructions, about 7 minutes. Reserve ¼ cup of the pasta cooking water and drain the pasta.

3

In a large bowl, combine the crème fraîche, lemon zest and juice, mint, basil, and remaining 2 tablespoons olive oil.

4

Add the pasta, chickpeas, roasted tomatoes, and fennel, and reserved ¼ cup pasta cooking liquid. Toss to coat the pasta and combine the ingredients. Season to taste with salt and pepper.

5

Serve or cover and refrigerate until ready to serve.

SERVES 6 to 8

SKILL LEVEL 2

2 tablespoons tahini

2 tablespoons fresh
lemon juice

½ teaspoon honey

1 garlic clove, finely grated

Kosher salt and freshly
ground black pepper

¼ cup olive oil

1 pound snow peas, trimmed,
strings removed, and halved

1 bunch radishes,
thinly sliced

1 bunch scallions, sliced
(about ¼ cup)

4 ounces feta cheese,
crumbled

Any extra tahini dressing can be stored in the fridge or drizzled over a grain bowl. Don't get lazy with the snow peas: Trimming the ends and pulling out the string that runs along the top means the difference between a tender salad and a tough one.

CRISPY SNOW PEAS WITH RADISHES, FETA, AND TAHINI DRESSING

1

In a large bowl, whisk together the tahini, lemon juice, honey, garlic, 1 tablespoon water, and season with salt and pepper. While whisking, drizzle in the oil and whisk to combine.

2

Add the snow peas, radishes, and scallions to the bowl with the tahini dressing. Toss to coat. Add the feta cheese and gently mix to combine. Serve.

Cherries and pistachios don't play together in desserts as often as they should, so we fix that here with a sweet, transportable finish for your picnic. But, as ever, go wild with your choice of jam or preserves, as long as your choice is not too thin. Jelly won't work, however, because it dissolves into fruit juice once it warms up.

SERVES 6 to 8
SKILL LEVEL 3

CHERRY PISTACHIO SHORTBREAD BARS

1¼ cups (2½ sticks) unsalted butter, cubed and chilled, plus room-temperature butter for greasing the pan

½ cup shelled pistachios

2 cups all-purpose flour

½ cup almond flour

½ cup sugar

2 teaspoons orange zest (from 1 orange)

1 teaspoon kosher salt

1 cup cherry preserves

1
Preheat the oven to 375°F. Line a 9-inch square baking pan with a long piece of parchment paper, so that the ends of the paper hang over the edges of the pan. Grease the parchment with butter.

2
In a food processor, pulse the pistachios until coarsely chopped. Remove half the pistachios and set aside. Add the flour, almond flour, sugar, orange zest, and salt to the food processor and pulse until a crumbly dough forms.

3
Press half the dough into the prepared pan, creating a ¼-inch-thick crust. Bake until the crust is lightly golden around the edges, 20 to 25 minutes.

4
In a medium bowl, mix together the remaining dough and the reserved pistachios; refrigerate while the crust bakes.

5
Spread the cherry preserves in an even layer over the baked crust. Crumble the dough-pistachio mixture over the preserves. Bake until the crumble topping is golden, 35 to 40 minutes. Cool for 15 minutes. Slice into squares and serve.

A Formal Affair

MENU

In the dead of winter, when everyone is bored stiff with their post-holiday detoxes and weekends wearing sweatpants, shoot a flare into the social wilderness with an unexpected invitation to a dress-up dinner party. Find an excuse to make everyone feel like a chic adult (is it someone's birthday, perhaps?), or don't: doesn't matter, it's time for some fun formality.

Make like your mom and pull out your "good china" and "hostess set" along with those natty napkin rings you stored, unopened, at the back of the linen closet promptly after receiving them. Disorient your digital friends with an analog (aka paper) invitation announcing "cocktail attire required" and get ready to field questions about what that means exactly.

All the outfit planning will raise expectations for your menu, but you know how to run the gauntlet. You'll reward your guests' efforts with classic dishes made modern using unexpected flavors, like a traditional chocolate cake flavored with cardamom. Even the limey gimlet gets a twist, with basil notes and tequila (rather than gin) as its base.

Sure, your formal affair will require more planning than usual, and the shopping list isn't cheap. But the return on your investment will be a warm winter evening that makes spring seem close enough to taste.

Skill Level

The duck takes some serious kitchen IQ—you know who should handle this one. The rest of the recipes—like the restaurant-style dishes that they are—require some last-minute finesse, so rally your guests to all pitch in together at the end.

Special Equipment

- Bundt pan or 8-inch round cake pan
- 12-inch cast-iron skillet
- Stand mixer
- Three 18 x 13–inch rimmed sheet pans

Game Plan

- **The Night Before:** Make the cake and the aioli
- **One Hour Before:** Make the potatoes
- **45 Minutes Before:** Make the toasts and duck
- **30 Minutes Before:** Make the salad and broccoli rabe
- **Right Before Serving:** Make the gimlets

Place potential matches beside each other and avoid co-locating sworn enemies or failed romances.

Wine Ideas

Sautéed mushrooms love a spiced, cherry-flavored Pinot Noir from Burgundy. Well, the duck with cherry sauce loves it too, but the Pinot won't play favorites in this menu. Try a dry Chenin Blanc from the Loire Valley with the winter salad to complement the dish's pleasant bitter note.

Pro-Tip:
Be a Social Engineer

Avoid dinnertime table-hovering by setting out place cards before guests arrive. Place potential matches beside each other and avoid co-locating sworn enemies or failed romances. Boisterous guests sit at the center, with an introvert to either side. Couples should be separated so that single friends don't feel scarlet-lettered. Self-obsessed bores should be placed at one end, preferably near a mirror, so they can admire themselves together without interrupting the fun. Your good-time Charlie goes nearest the bar where he can keep the drinks flowing throughout dinner. And naturally you sit at the spot closest to the kitchen. If anyone is bringing a guest whose name you don't know in advance, keep blank cards at the ready and stealthily finish the card after introductions are made. "Guest of X" doesn't seem very welcoming.

Pro-Tip:
Appetizer Blueprint

The mushroom toasts in this menu offer an appetizer blueprint whose concept you should master: In a pinch, you can always concoct a winning appetizer by mounding just about any well-seasoned sauté of tender veggies atop slices of toasted sourdough (or even baguette). If the veggies are boring, include cheese on the toast (below the veg or crumbled atop).

In this menu, we lighten a mix of earthy mushrooms with bright green parsley and mint. But the same herbs and seasoning could easily be stirred into a quick sauté of grated zucchini. Or sauté mushrooms and chopped kale with a bit of crushed garlic and pile it high on a smear of Brie on a little toast. The variations are endless, as are search engine results for the phrase "toast topping variations."

Party Math:
What Booze Should I Buy?

Want to skip the signature cocktail in one of these menus and offer guests simple mixed drinks (like tequila-soda or gin-tonic) instead? Here are the must-haves for a respectable basic bar:

- **Spirits:** A bottle each of vodka, gin, tequila, bourbon, and white rum will make the basic classics. Choose brands according to your budget (remember that house brands from discount retailers like Costco, Aldi, and Lidl win blind taste-test awards against premium brands all the time). Afraid of looking cheap? Buy classy glass decanters on eBay to disguise your thrift.

- **Must-Have Mixers:** Club soda, tonic, and ginger ale or ginger beer

- **Optional Mixers:** Sweet vermouth (for Manhattans and variations), dry vermouth (for martinis), bitters (for mixed drink je ne sais quoi), triple sec (for margaritas), and orange juice (for gin-and-juice, duh)

- **Garnishes:** Lemons, limes, and pitted olives

- **Goods:** Just about any mixed drink can be unpretentiously enjoyed from a basic 8- to 10-ounce rocks glass. Stock 1½ glasses (and 1½ cocktail napkins) per guest per hour.

- **Ice:** Stock 1 pound per guest per hour, which covers drinking as well as chilling beer.

Disorient your digital friends with an analog (aka paper) invitation announcing "cocktail attire required" and get ready to field questions about what that means exactly.

Basil adds an unexpected floral flavor to these sophisticated cocktails, but don't skip the sieving step unless you want to stare at small green flecks in your guests' teeth for the rest of the night. Tacky.

MAKES 12 cocktails
SKILL LEVEL 2

BASIL TEQUILA GIMLETS

2½ cups basil leaves, plus more for garnish

¾ cup simple syrup

1 cup plus 2 tablespoons fresh lime juice

3 cups silver tequila

Ice

1
In a large pitcher, muddle the basil with ¼ cup of the simple syrup. Add the remaining simple syrup and the lime juice, then stir to incorporate.

2
Strain through a fine-mesh sieve into a clean pitcher and serve with the tequila, a cocktail jigger, shakers, a bowl of ice, chilled coupe glasses, and extra basil leaves alongside for your guests to serve themselves.

3
For each cocktail, combine 1¼ ounces of the lime mixture and 2 ounces of the tequila in a shaker and fill with ice. Shake vigorously until chilled, then strain the liquid into a chilled coupe glass, garnish with a basil leaf, and serve.

If your bread loaf is too large, cut the slices in half to ensure a handheld portion size; we're not making open-faced sandwiches here.

SAUTÉED MUSHROOMS AND FRESH HERB TOASTS

4 tablespoons plus 1 teaspoon extra-virgin olive oil

4 tablespoons (½ stick) unsalted butter

2 medium shallots, minced

2 pounds cremini mushrooms, cleaned and thinly sliced

Leaves from 4 sprigs thyme

Kosher salt

8 slices whole wheat sourdough bread

1 cup loosely packed fresh parsley leaves

½ cup loosely packed fresh mint leaves

½ teaspoon red pepper flakes

1 garlic clove, halved

Zest and juice of 1 lemon

Sea salt

1

In a large nonstick skillet, heat 2 tablespoons each of the olive oil and butter over medium heat. Add half the shallots and cook, stirring occasionally, until soft, about 2 minutes.

2

Add half the sliced mushrooms, half the thyme, and a pinch of kosher salt and cook, stirring very occasionally, until the mushrooms are brown and tender, about 6 minutes. Transfer the cooked mushrooms and shallots to a bowl. Repeat the process with 2 tablespoons of the oil, and the remaining 2 tablespoons butter, shallots, and mushrooms, adding the finished sautéed mushrooms and shallots to the bowl with the rest.

3

Toast the bread lightly in a toaster or on a sheet pan in a preheated 450°F oven.

4

Meanwhile, in a medium bowl, toss the parsley, mint, red pepper flakes, and remaining 1 teaspoon olive oil.

5

Rub the toasts lightly with the garlic clove, then discard it. Spoon the mushrooms on top of the toasts. Top with the dressed herbs, lemon zest and juice, and a pinch of sea salt.

We roll our eyes at those design-minded friends who claim that anything off-white and black, minimalist, and overpriced is "on trend" (they're just not sophisticated enough to work with color or coupons). But we'll make an exception for this nearly monochromatic salad of pale endive, ivory dressing, and matte brown almonds. It's dead-chic . . . with a sprinkle of Aleppo pepper, because we know how.

SERVES 8
SKILL LEVEL 2

1 medium shallot, finely minced

1 tablespoon white wine vinegar

1 cup full-fat plain yogurt (regular, not Greek*)

4 tablespoons extra-virgin olive oil

Kosher salt and freshly ground black pepper

4 Belgian endives, trimmed and separated into individual leaves

½ cup sliced almonds, toasted

Aleppo pepper, for garnish

WINTER SALAD WITH ALMONDS AND ALEPPO PEPPER

1

Combine the shallot and vinegar in a medium bowl and let sit for 10 minutes. Stir in the yogurt, 2 tablespoons of the olive oil, and salt and pepper to taste. If the dressing is not a pourable consistency, add the remaining olive oil a little at a time to thin it.

2

When ready to serve, arrange the endives on a platter, spoon the yogurt dressing over them, and top with the toasted almonds. Sprinkle some Aleppo pepper on top, if you like, and serve.

*If you only have Greek on hand, you can use a couple of tablespoons of buttermilk to thin it out to a pourable consistency.

Duck has an intimidating reputation for many home cooks, but it's actually quite simple to prepare. Our oven technique helps to avoid overcooking the duck meat while still delivering a crispy skin. A spiced cherry sauce imparts a savory-sweet communion that will make converts of any of the duck-dubious at your table. Note: Don't cook the dish until about 45 minutes before you want to serve it, and don't wash the skillet until after you make the sauce.

SERVES 8
SKILL LEVEL 5

ROASTED DUCK BREAST WITH SPICED CHERRY SAUCE

FOR THE DUCK

8 medium duck breasts
(8 to 10 ounces each)

2 tablespoons finely ground
star anise (ground in a spice
grinder)

Kosher salt

FOR THE CHERRY SAUCE

6 tablespoons (¾ stick)
unsalted butter

1 shallot, minced

1 star anise pod

1 cinnamon stick

2 (24-ounce) jars sour
cherries, drained

1¼ cups chicken broth

1 cup tawny port

¼ cup honey

Kosher salt and coarsely
ground black pepper

1

MAKE THE DUCK: Preheat the oven to 450°F.

2

Pat the duck breasts dry with a paper towel. Using a sharp knife, cut a ½-inch crosshatch pattern into the skin, taking care not to penetrate deeper than the thick layer of fat under the skin. Season only the meat side generously with the star anise and salt.

3

Place half the duck breasts skin-side down into a cold 12-inch cast-iron skillet (they should not be crowded) and set the skillet over medium-high heat. Cook the duck breasts without flipping until the skin is crispy and the fat has rendered, 5 to 6 minutes. Transfer the breasts to a sheet pan, skin-side up. Let the skillet cool completely, then repeat to cook the remaining duck breasts and transfer them to the pan with the others. Do not clean the skillet. Roast the duck breasts on the sheet pan in the oven until the center of each breast reaches 130°F, about 10 minutes.

RECIPE CONTINUES

4

MAKE THE CHERRY SAUCE:
Meanwhile, discard all but
1 tablespoon of the rendered
fat from the skillet you used
to brown the duck. Add the
butter, shallot, star anise,
and cinnamon stick and
sauté over medium heat
until the shallot is tender.

5

Chop ¼ cup of the cherries
and set aside. Add the
remaining whole cherries,
the broth, and port to the
skillet and cook until the
cherries have softened and
the liquid has reduced, about
10 minutes. Remove the
cinnamon stick and star
anise. Pour the cherry sauce
and honey into a blender (or
use an immersion blender
directly in the skillet) and
blend until smooth. Season
to taste with salt and
pepper.

6

Place the cooked duck
breasts skin-side up on a
cutting board and rest for
10 minutes. Carve each
breast against the grain
into 4 or 5 pieces for easy
serving. Serve with the
spiced cherry sauce drizzled
over the top, and garnished
with the reserved chopped
cherries.

Build a Bar

- Apply user-centered design by laying out supplies and ingredients in the order they'll be required: first glassware, then ice, then cocktail components, then garnishes, and finally napkins.

- Glasses don't have to match! Cluster an assortment of mix-and-match glassware like the eccentric entertainer you are.

- Avoid stack attacks by laying glasses in a single layer if there's room.

- Cocktail mixing is a mess: Protect valuable surfaces with a tablecloth over a hidden plastic liner.

- Typical ice buckets are too small for a party and require constant refilling. Use a large bowl or beverage tub and don't forget a scoop or slotted spoon.

- Ice bowls pool water at their bases, so place kitchen towels underneath or invest in a beverage tub with a fluted foot.

Aioli is just a fancy word for mayonnaise. It often includes garlic, but we've replaced it here with the sharp tang of mustard. Draped in ribbons over mashed potatoes, it takes an otherwise humble dish over the top. Note: The USDA doesn't recommend consuming raw egg, which this recipe contains.

AIOLI MASHED POTATOES WITH CHIVES AND PIMENT D'ESPELETTE

FOR THE AIOLI

2 large egg yolks

1 tablespoon Dijon mustard

Kosher salt

1½ cups canola oil

FOR THE MASHED POTATOES

3 pounds baby Yukon Gold or baby red potatoes, unpeeled

2 fresh bay leaves

Kosher salt

¼ cup extra-virgin olive oil

2 tablespoons finely chopped fresh chives, for garnish

Piment d'Espelette or red pepper flakes, for garnish

1

MAKE THE AIOLI: Using a large whisk, beat the egg yolks, 2 tablespoons water, the mustard, and salt in a medium glass bowl until well combined. (To keep the bowl from sliding around your countertop, you can drape a kitchen towel over a small saucepan, then set the bowl over it so it stays in place.) Whisking constantly, gradually drizzle in the oil, drop by drop, until the sauce begins to emulsify and thicken. Continue adding the oil in a steady stream, whisking constantly, until all the oil has been incorporated. If you're not using the aioli soon, cover and chill it, but bring it to room temperature before using. (The aioli can be made a day ahead and stored in the refrigerator.)

2

MAKE THE MASHED POTATOES: Place the potatoes and bay leaves in a large pot and cover with cold water by 2 inches. Season the water generously with salt and bring to a boil. Reduce the heat to maintain a simmer and cook until the potatoes are very tender, 18 to 25 minutes. Drain, reserving ½ cup of the cooking liquid, and let the potatoes stand until dry. Discard the bay leaves.

3

Place the potatoes back into the pot. Using a potato masher or wooden spoon, smash the potatoes against the side of the pot. Add the reserved ½ cup cooking liquid and the olive oil and continue smashing and

RECIPE CONTINUES

stirring vigorously until combined. (The potatoes can be made up to this point up to 5 hours in advance.) Place the pot over medium heat and cook, stirring, until the potatoes have warmed through, 2 to 3 minutes. Remove the potatoes from the heat and stir in half the aioli. The potatoes should look very creamy.

4

Transfer the potatoes to a serving dish and drizzle with additional aioli to taste. Garnish with the chives and piment d'Espelette or red pepper flakes. Serve warm.

Dinner Party Playlists

A good dinner party becomes a great dinner party when it's set to a soundtrack that subtly contorts your guests' moods and energy levels to the phases of the party, from chill arrival to boisterous farewell. Music sets your party's tone and tempo—literally!—so don't treat it like background noise. Prep a three- to four-hour playlist that starts calmly (your guests will be acclimating for the first thirty minutes), sparkles steadily for ninety minutes of eating and then takes off just as your guests need motivation to get up and mingle again. Mix some unexpected hits into the set list and don't forget a corny sing-along toward the end of the night when inhibitions are low.

Too busy to prep a playlist yourself? Ask your friend who still talks about their glory days as a late-night college radio station DJ to bring the playlist as their contribution to the party. No music obsessives in your crew? Then turn to any of the packaged playlists on offer from Spotify or Apple Music.

Here are some of our favorites:

1. "Classic Rock Dinner Party," on both Spotify and Apple Music, is for a night with your high school buddies: Van Morrison, Luther Vandross, Talking Heads, along with some potential classics from the likes of Aloe Blacc and the Scissor Sisters.

2. "Hipster Cocktail Party," on Spotify, is all over the musical map, from Sinatra and Fitzgerald to Bob Marley to Wilco and Vampire Weekend and beyond. But, somehow, it works!

3. "Rooftop Cocktail Party," on Spotify, is designed to ensure that your guests will be ready to move the party indoors once the rooftop closes, packed with vibey hits that nearly everyone will recognize from the last decade or so.

4. "Teen Dance Party," on Spotify, or "Teen Party," on Apple Music, don't need much elaboration. Just know that "teen" is a musical state of mind and not an ageist warning label here.

5. "80s Rock Hits," on Spotify, or "80s Smash Hits," on Apple Music, is your later-night go-to in the event that energy levels are waning or the party atmosphere feels off. Everyone's glad to be at your place when Toto's "Africa" helps them "hear the drums echoing tonight." So, turn it up and let's pour another.

Broccoli's cynical cousin, broccoli rabe, is one of those guys you must handle gently to avoid a bitter result. A light toss in oil and a quick roast will make it play nicely with humble chickpeas in this Indian-inspired side dish that echoes the flavors you introduced with the gimlet and its basil. This is also an opportunity to remember that not all guests like everything: While you're not required to cook around everyone's individual tastes, you also shouldn't guilt your guests into trying the broccoli rabe out of fear of hurting your feelings.

SERVES 8
SKILL LEVEL 2

ROASTED BROCCOLI RABE AND CHICKPEAS

1 (15-ounce) can chickpeas, drained, rinsed, and patted dry

5 tablespoons extra-virgin olive oil

2 teaspoons cumin seeds

¼ teaspoon red pepper flakes

Kosher salt

2 bunches broccoli rabe, bottom third of the stems removed

1 lemon, cut into wedges, for serving

1
Preheat the oven to 450°F.

2
Place the chickpeas, 2 tablespoons of the olive oil, the cumin seeds, red pepper flakes, and a pinch of salt in a large bowl and toss. Divide the dressed chickpeas between two sheet pans. Roast the chickpeas for 15 minutes, or until crispy.

3
Meanwhile, put the broccoli rabe, the remaining 3 tablespoons oil, and a pinch of salt in the same large bowl and toss. When the chickpeas are crispy, lay the broccoli rabe in a single layer on top of them, return the pans to the hot oven, and roast for about 8 minutes, or until the broccoli rabe stems are tender.

4
Serve hot, with lemon wedges on the side for squeezing.

The 1990s called—they want their Molten chocolate cake back. Opt instead for this dark crowd-pleaser that will scent the kitchen with a floral cardamom perfume while it bakes. Serve with generous champagne pours.

Note: Make the cake first so the oven is free to make the duck later. No Bundt pan? Use an 8-inch round pan that's at least 3 inches deep, and bake the cake for an hour.

CHOCOLATE CARDAMOM CAKE WITH WALNUT CREAM

SERVES 8
SKILL LEVEL 3

FOR THE CHOCOLATE CARDAMOM CAKE

Unsalted butter, at room temperature, for the pans

¾ cup unsweetened Dutch-process cocoa powder, plus more for the pan

1½ cups all-purpose flour

1½ cups granulated sugar

1½ teaspoons ground cardamom

1½ teaspoons baking soda

¾ teaspoon baking powder

¾ teaspoon kosher salt

2 large eggs

¾ cup whole milk

3 tablespoons vegetable oil

FOR THE WALNUT CREAM

2 cups cold heavy cream

2 tablespoons walnut oil

1 teaspoon granulated sugar

Powdered sugar, for dusting

1

MAKE THE CAKE: Preheat the oven to 350°F. Butter a 10-cup Bundt pan and dust it with cocoa powder.

2

Sift the cocoa powder, flour, granulated sugar, cardamom, baking soda, baking powder, and salt into the bowl of a stand mixer fitted with the whisk attachment. Beat on low speed until just combined. Raise the speed to medium and add the eggs, milk, oil, and ¾ cup water. Beat for about 3 minutes, until the batter is smooth.

3

Pour the batter into the prepared pan and bake until a toothpick inserted into the center comes out clean,

about 40 minutes. Let the cake cool slightly in the pan, then invert the cake on the wire rack and allow to cool completely.

4

MAKE THE WALNUT CREAM: Meanwhile, clean the mixer bowl and fit the mixer with the whisk attachment. Pour the cream, walnut oil (if using), and granulated sugar into the mixer bowl and whip until the cream holds soft peaks. Refrigerate until serving.

5

Dust the cake with powdered sugar, slice, and serve with a big dollop of the cream.

Dinner and a Movie

MENU

This menu is designed for a cozy evening at home with a few folks you know well enough already. Dinner and a movie is the move when you're already caught up but want to hang with close neighbors, your sister and her roommate, or the couple you just met on vacation. There's a simple rye-thyme lemonade to toast the no-agenda gathering, but the real special sauce for this easy evening is a well-timed braise. You'll gather your group early to prep the meal, then pop the "hunter's stew" into the oven and settle down to a favorite flick while passing lemon–poppy seed popcorn.

Excuse yourself halfway through to put the pretzel monkey bread into the oven, and set things up to roast the apples as soon as the credits roll. Then it's time to enjoy some armchair criticism and post-flick debate . . . until the baked apple dessert, that is. Then it's time to just enjoy.

Skill Level

The monkey bread requires deep admin–level skills; put your engineer friend on it. Assign a twosome to the bigos—it requires a lot of prep, but it's set-it-and-forget-it once in the oven. The rest of the crew can handle the popcorn and apples.

Special Equipment

- 9-inch round metal cake pan

- Punch bowl

- Stand mixer

- 9-inch square baking dish or pie dish

Game Plan

- **Three Hours Before:** Make the monkey bread

- **Two Hours Before:** Make the bigos

- **One Hour Before:** Bake the apples

- **45 Minutes Before:** Make the lemonade

- **30 Minutes Before:** Make the popcorn and reheat the monkey bread

This menu is designed for a cozy evening at home with a few folks you know well enough already.

Wine Ideas

A silky and citrusy Arneis from Italy is a fresh and bright pairing with the sweet-and-salty popcorn, if you want to skip the cocktail. A hearty and dark-fruited Barbera from the Piedmont is perfect for the bigos.

1 bunch thyme

1 (12-ounce) can frozen lemonade concentrate, defrosted

1½ cups rye whiskey

Ice

Orange bitters (optional)

1 lemon, cut into wheels, for garnish

Earthy rye checks the "cozy" box in this menu, and lemonade says, "but not boring!" This cocktail is also a winner because you can do the measuring in the empty frozen lemonade can to avoid dirtying one extra dish.

RYE-THYME LEMONADE

1

Wrap the bunch of thyme in a coffee filter or a piece of cheesecloth and secure it with a piece of string. Make sure the leaves are all enclosed in the filter or cheescloth; otherwise, they will come loose and float around in the punch. Set aside.

2

Empty the lemonade concentrate into a large punch bowl. Fill the empty lemonade can with rye (1½ cups) and add it to the bowl. Using the same lemonade can, measure 3 cans of water into the bowl (4½ cups total). Stir until the lemonade concentrate is completely mixed in. Add the thyme sachet and let sit for at least 30 minutes.

3

When ready to serve, remove and discard the thyme sachet. Serve the drink over ice, with a dash or two of orange bitters on top of each drink, if desired, and garnish with a lemon wheel.

This recipe may sound like a classic flavor profile often reserved for coffee shop muffins, but you'll be done for good with boring old buttered popcorn once you get a taste of this salty-sweet masterpiece.

SERVES 4
SKILL LEVEL 1

SWEET-AND-SALTY LEMON–POPPY SEED POPCORN

½ cup olive oil

1 cup white popcorn kernels

4 teaspoons grated lemon zest

2 teaspoons sea salt

2 teaspoons sugar

6 tablespoons (¾ stick) unsalted butter

2 tablespoons fresh lemon juice

2 tablespoons poppy seeds

1

In a very large heavy-bottomed pot, heat the oil over medium-high heat for 1 to 2 minutes. Add the popcorn kernels and swirl the pot to coat the kernels in the oil. Cover with a lid and cook until the kernels stop popping, about 6 minutes.

2

In a small bowl, combine the lemon zest, sea salt, and sugar. Using the back of a wooden spoon, press the ingredients together to infuse with the zest.

3

In a small pot, melt the butter. Remove from the heat and add the lemon juice and the sugar mixture.

4

Transfer the popcorn to a large serving bowl. Pour the lemon butter and the poppy seeds over the popcorn. Toss to evenly coat. Serve immediately.

¼ ounce dried porcini mushrooms (½ cup)

2 cups boiling water

1 tablespoon olive oil

½ pound double-smoked slab bacon, cut into ½-inch pieces

1 pound smoked kielbasa, cut into 1½-inch pieces

1 to 1½ pounds pork butt, cut into 1½-inch cubes

Kosher salt

1 large yellow onion, thinly sliced

3 garlic cloves, thinly sliced

Freshly ground black pepper

2 tablespoons tomato paste

2 pounds sauerkraut, drained

½ cup pitted prunes, chopped

1 teaspoon juniper berries

1 teaspoon whole cloves

2 bay leaves

2 cups chicken stock

1 cup dry white wine

8 ounces small red new potatoes, halved

Assorted mustards, for serving

Since this stew cooks for two hours, you can prep it with the rest of the dishes, pop it into the oven, and then go watch that movie. Once the final credits roll, you'll just need to add the potatoes and warm up the bread.

BIGOS (POLISH PORK STEW)

1

In a small bowl, cover the dried mushrooms with the boiling water. Let steep for 15 minutes. Using a slotted spoon, transfer the mushrooms to a cutting board and chop them. Strain the mushroom soaking liquid to remove any grit and set aside.

2

In a 6- or 8-quart Dutch oven, heat the oil over medium heat. Working in batches, cook the bacon and kielbasa until browned and slightly crisped, 8 to 10 minutes. Using a slotted spoon, transfer them to a plate and repeat to cook the remaining bacon and kielbasa.

3

Season the pork butt with 1 teaspoon salt. Add to the pot and cook, turning as needed, until golden brown on all sides, 6 to 8 minutes. Transfer to a plate.

4

To the same pot, add the onion and garlic, and season with ½ teaspoon salt and a few grinds of pepper. Cook until lightly browned, about 5 minutes. Add the tomato paste and cook, stirring, for 1 minute. Add the sauerkraut, prunes, juniper berries, cloves, and bay leaves. Cook until warmed through and fragrant, about 3 minutes. Add the bacon, kielbasa, pork butt, stock, and white wine. Bring to a simmer and cook, with the lid ajar, until the pork butt is tender, about 2 hours.

5

Add the potatoes, chopped mushrooms, and mushroom soaking liquid; cook until the potatoes are tender, about 15 minutes. Season the stew with salt and pepper to taste.

6

Serve the stew with mustard.

If you're making the whole menu, start the dough first. This pull-apart bread can also be baked an hour or two before dinner and reheated for a few minutes in a 200°F oven before being drizzled with the garlic butter.

SERVES 4
SKILL LEVEL 5

PRETZEL MONKEY BREAD WITH GARLIC BUTTER

1 teaspoon active dry yeast

1 cup warm water (between 100 and 115°F)

1 tablespoon firmly packed dark brown sugar

3¼ cups unbleached bread flour

6 tablespoons (¾ stick) unsalted butter, at room temperature

2 teaspoons kosher salt

Nonstick baking spray

½ cup baking soda

2 garlic cloves, finely minced

1 tablespoon finely minced fresh flat-leaf parsley

1

Sprinkle the yeast over the warm water in the bowl of a stand mixer or in a large bowl. Stir in the brown sugar until it's dissolved. Allow the yeast to bloom until foamy, about 5 minutes.

2

Add the flour, 2 tablespoons of the butter, and 1½ teaspoons of the salt to the yeast mixture and stir to form a shaggy mass. Using the dough hook attachment of the stand mixer, knead the dough on medium-high speed. After about 1 minute, the dough will form a smooth ball, quite firm and slightly tacky but not sticky. If it is sticky, add a little more flour, a tablespoon at a time, and knead until smooth. If the dough is too dry to come together, add more water, 1 teaspoon at a time, and knead until smooth. Continue kneading the dough until it is elastic, 5 to 7 minutes more. (Alternatively, turn the shaggy dough out onto an unfloured work surface and knead it by hand.)

3

Coat a medium bowl with nonstick spray, place the dough in it, and cover it tightly with plastic wrap. Put the bowl in a warm place and allow the dough to rise until doubled in size, 45 minutes to 1 hour.

4

Preheat the oven to 450°F. Line a 9-inch round metal cake pan with parchment paper and spray the parchment with nonstick spray.

RECIPE CONTINUES

5

Turn the dough out onto an unfloured work surface and firmly press it down to deflate. Cut the dough into 20 pieces, each about the same size. Set aside, uncovered, for 5 to 10 minutes while you prepare the baking soda bath.

6

Combine the baking soda and 6 cups water in a wide stainless-steel saucepan and bring to a simmer over high heat. Decrease the heat to maintain a gentle simmer, and add half the dough pieces. Simmer for about 30 seconds, then lift the dough from the water using a large skimmer, allowing the excess liquid to drain. Transfer the dough to the prepared pan. Repeat with the remaining dough pieces, nestling them in the pan with the first batch so you have one snug layer.

7

Bake until the tops of the little pretzel balls are deeply browned, about 12 minutes.

8

Meanwhile, melt the remaining 4 tablespoons butter in a small saucepan over medium heat. Add the garlic and remaining ½ teaspoon salt. Simmer for 2 minutes, then remove the pan from the heat. Stir in the parsley and keep warm.

9

When the monkey bread is done, lift the bread from the pan using the edges of the parchment and transfer the whole thing to a large round serving platter. Slide the parchment out from underneath and discard it. Drizzle the garlic butter over the top, letting it pool in the crevices and drip down the sides of the bread. Serve warm.

½ cup (1 stick) unsalted butter

4 large apples, such as Rome or Empire

½ cup pecans, toasted and chopped

½ cup packed light brown sugar

½ teaspoon pumpkin pie spice

½ teaspoon kosher salt

1 pint vanilla ice cream, for serving

This classic autumn dessert gets a subtle upgrade with pumpkin pie spice and a vanilla ice cream accompaniment. If you're over the pumpkin-spice-everything fad, just use cinnamon.

BROWN BUTTER PECAN-STUFFED BAKED APPLES WITH VANILLA ICE CREAM

1

Preheat the oven to 350°F. Lightly grease a 9-inch square baking dish or pie dish with 1 tablespoon of the butter.

2

Using an apple corer or paring knife, remove the cores from the apples starting from the stem end. Leave the bottoms of the apples intact. Transfer the apples to the prepared baking dish.

3

In a small saucepan, melt the remaining butter over medium-high heat. Cook until the milk solids in the butter begin to brown, about 4 minutes. Remove from the heat. Stir in the pecans, brown sugar, pumpkin pie spice, and salt.

4

Transfer the pecan mixture to a small bowl. Cover and chill in the refrigerator for at least 15 minutes.

5

Fill each apple with the pecan mixture. Bake until the apples are tender, about 45 minutes. If the sugar on top starts to burn, cover the pan with aluminum foil.

6

Serve the warm baked apples with a scoop of vanilla ice cream on the side.

An All-Day Brunch

MENU

This party should technically begin around noon and end three hours later. But when you invite your cabin-feverish friends for an early-afternoon "brunch" of colorful, Nordic-inspired fare on one of the first nice Saturdays of spring, the casual get-together that was supposed to be a post-gym, pre-laundry pit stop will turn into such a good time (and that weather—unbeatable!) that guests will linger much longer than they intended.

Eventually afternoon plans will be relocated to your place, as friends of your friends stop by to sip iced coffee cocktails and admire the baked side of salmon. Your room-temp-friendly cardamom oatmeal can go the distance, though, and the Scandinavian smorrebrod sandwiches are easily re-merchandised when uninvited neighbors randomly appear.

Suddenly, afternoon is early evening and someone's girlfriend is filling your dishwasher. A latecomer arrives with more ice and IPAs to replenish the bar, while buzzed buddies text typo-laden cancellations to their dinner dates. Because who could imagine anywhere better to be than at your day-to-night brunch, catching up on everything with everyone and worrying about nothing and no one . . . except perhaps the lemon curd pavlova that was gobbled up hours ago.

The lights will lower as pizza arrives for a thinning crowd of die-hards and true believers. And you'll deservedly sigh to yourself with a bit of self-satisfaction, because you single-handedly sprung spring.

Skill Level

This menu will go more smoothly if you start on the oatmeal and pavlova the night before. So why not invite a couple of friends over for a nightcap-slash-mini-prep party?

Special Equipment

- Stand mixer

- 8-inch square baking dish

- Two 18 x 13–inch rimmed sheet pans

Game Plan

- **The Night Before:** Prepare the oatmeal and bake the pavlova

- **Two Hours Before:** Make the smorrebrod and bake the salmon

- **One Hour Before:** Bake the oatmeal

- **45 Minutes Before:** Finish the pavlova and make the asparagus

- **30 Minutes Before:** Make the cold brew

Wine Ideas

Keep it light and refreshing with a citrusy and minerally Grüner Veltliner from Austria for the eggs and asparagus. Serve a crisp and dry Provençal rosé to lighten the tone on the baked salmon.

Pro-Tip:
Brunch for the Broke

On a tight budget or feeling overspent but still have the urge (or obligation) to gather friends? Brunch is one of the most cost-effective ways to entertain, since you can pull it off well without an expensive trip to the butcher. Eggs, milk, and cheese dominate a brunch shopping list, and it's totally cool to offer only wine and beer (skipping the hard-spirit cocktails). Or ask your friends to bring the libations. Either way, you can afford a good time for your crew for less than half what a classic dinner party costs.

Brunch is one of the most cost-effective ways to entertain, since you can pull it off well without an expensive trip to the butcher.

Cold-brewed coffee is naturally bitter, so choose an amaro that is lighter-bodied and sweet, like Averna or Nonino. Avoid more bitter options like Fernet, Braulio, or Montenegro for this cocktail (though those are delicious on their own).

MAKES 8 to 10 cocktails
SKILL LEVEL 3

1 tablespoon ground cinnamon

½ cup raw sugar

Lemon wedges for rimming the glasses

20 ounces cold-brewed coffee (we like Stumptown cold brew)

1 cup amaro (we like Averna for its medium body and sweetness but any amaro will do)

¾ cup silver mezcal

¼ cup fresh lemon juice

Ice

Whipped cream (optional)

Espresso powder (optional)

COLD-BREW COCKTAIL

1
Combine the cinnamon and raw sugar on a plate. Prep your glasses by rubbing a lemon wedge around the rim and dipping the wet rim into the sugar mixture to coat. Set aside.

2
OPTION 1: Combine the cold brew, amaro, mezcal, and lemon juice in a large carafe. Set up a shaker station with ice and a strainer next to the carafe. When it comes time to serve, pour about ½ cup of the mixture per serving into the shaker (you can usually fit two cocktails per shaker), fill with ice, and

shake vigorously until frothy. Pour into two of the prepared glasses and top with whipped cream and espresso powder, if desired. Repeat to make additional cocktails in batches of two.

3
OPTION 2: Combine the cold brew, amaro, mezcal, and lemon juice in a blender. Add 2 cups ice and blend until frothy and cold (it should still be sippable, not thick like a frappé). Pour into the prepared glasses and top with whipped cream and espresso powder, if desired.

Smorrebrod just means "open-faced sandwich," so even novices can help assemble these beauts. Make at least two variations for visual effect, or stick to just one if you're pinched for time.

SMORREBROD
• ROASTED GRAPE
• RICOTTA-PEAR
• EDAMAME-MINT

FOR THE ROASTED GRAPE SMORREBROD

1 bunch red seedless grapes (about 1 pound)

2 teaspoons olive oil

6 sprigs thyme

Kosher salt and freshly ground black pepper

Unsalted butter, at room temperature

3 slices thin-cut pumpernickel bread

4 ounces soft goat cheese

3 tablespoons crushed pistachios

FOR THE RICOTTA-PEAR SMORREBROD

Unsalted butter, at room temperature

3 slices thin-cut pumpernickel bread

½ cup ricotta

1 to 2 Anjou pears (about 10 ounces total), thinly sliced

Honey

Coarsely cracked black pepper

INGREDIENTS CONTINUE

1

MAKE THE ROASTED GRAPE SMORREBROD: Preheat the oven to 425°F.

2

Remove the grapes from their stems. In a small roasting pan, toss the grapes with the olive oil, thyme sprigs, salt, and pepper. Roast until the grapes have popped open but are still holding shape, about 10 minutes. Discard the thyme and let the grapes cool slightly.

3

Butter each slice of bread liberally, spread with 3 tablespoons of the goat cheese, top with about 15 roasted grapes (leaving behind their liquid), and sprinkle with 1 tablespoon of the pistachios. Cut each open-faced sandwich into a rectangle, removing the crusts; then cut the rectangle into evenly sized "fingers."

4

MAKE THE RICOTTA-PEAR SMORREBROD: Butter each slice of bread liberally, spread with about 3 table-spoons of the ricotta, top with the sliced pear to cover, then drizzle with honey and sprinkle with pepper. Cut each open-faced sandwich into a rectangle, removing the crusts; then cut the rectangle into evenly sized "fingers."

5

MAKE THE EDAMAME-MINT SMORREBROD: In a medium pan, combine the edamame, 3 tablespoons water, 1 tablespoon of the butter, the garlic, and the red pepper flakes. Cook over medium heat until tender, about 25 minutes. Crush the edamame mixture with a fork or process briefly in a food processor and add lemon juice to taste.

6

Butter each slice of bread with 1 tablespoon of the remaining butter, top with one third of the edamame mixture, tile the radishes on top, and garnish with an occasional mint leaf. Cut each open-faced sandwich into a rectangle, removing the crusts; then cut the rectangle into evenly sized "fingers."

FOR THE EDAMAME-MINT SMORREBROD

8 ounces frozen shelled edamame (about 1½ cups)

4 tablespoons (½ stick) salted butter

2 garlic cloves, coarsely chopped

Pinch of red pepper flakes

Lemon juice

3 slices thin-cut pumpernickel bread

3 radishes (about 3 ounces), thinly sliced

Mint leaves, for garnish

Smorrebrod How-To

These open-faced sandwiches may well be considered the national food of Denmark, and typically feature toppings that bend Scandinavian (think smoked or pickled fish, hard cheeses, beets, and dill). But the recent rage for all things Nordic has introduced iterations that stray far from the traditional Danish larder. You can apply a wide range of toppings with few restrictions and a couple of simple guidelines.

Start with thick slices of untoasted pumpernickel or rye bread (the denser and darker, the better) and spackle them with a generous layer of the best quality butter you can get your hands on. You can stop there (smorrebrod comes from the Danish words for butter and bread, and the dish itself requires nothing more), or treat it as a foundation for innumerable happy combinations. If you want to be fancy, slice off the edges—once the toppings are on—to make perfectly symmetrical borders.

No matter how early you plan to wake up to prepare for your brunch, it will be 30 minutes later than you should have. Hence this oatmeal hack: You can prep the recipe completely, then store it, covered, in the fridge overnight until you're ready to bake. Pop it in the oven for an hour before serving and you're set.

SERVES 6 to 8
SKILL LEVEL 3

BAKED OATMEAL WITH BLACKBERRIES

1½ cups steel-cut oats

2 quarts boiling water

½ cup chopped toasted walnuts

4 tablespoons (½ stick) unsalted butter, cubed, plus more for the pan

½ cup light brown sugar

1 cup whole milk

1 large egg

1 egg yolk

1 teaspoon ground cardamom

1 teaspoon kosher salt

12 ounces fresh or frozen blackberries (about 2 cups), plus more for garnish

Whipped cream, for serving

1

In a large bowl, cover the oats with the boiling water and soak for 6 hours. (Alternatively, soak the oats in room-temperature water overnight.)

2

In a small bowl, work the walnuts, butter, and ¼ cup of the brown sugar together. Refrigerate until cold, about 1 hour, or up to overnight.

3

After the oats are fully soaked, preheat the oven to 350°F. Butter an 8-inch square baking dish.

4

Drain the oats well and combine with the milk, egg, egg yolk, remaining ¼ cup brown sugar, cardamom, and salt. Scatter the blackberries over the bottom of the baking dish and cover with the oat mixture. Distribute the nut crumble evenly over the oats. Bake for 1 hour, or until nicely browned. To serve, top with whipped cream and fresh berries.

Pin bones are an unavoidable nuisance to both cook and eater. Even a dedicated fishmonger will leave them behind, so it's up to you to go the last mile and make sure the fish is free from choking hazards.

You should be able to see the tips of the tiny bones poking through the top of the salmon flesh, but if they're not immediately visible, run your fingers along the fish and you'll feel their hidden locations. Use a pair of needle-nose pliers (or clean tweezers, in a pinch) to pull each out in the direction in which they're oriented (you'll tear up the fish if you pull straight up or back). Be patient and make sure you have a firm grip on each one before tugging, or you'll risk breaking the bones and losing them for good.

SERVES 6 to 8
SKILL LEVEL 4

FOR THE HORSERADISH CREAM

3 tablespoons drained prepared horseradish

2 teaspoons fresh lemon juice

1 cup crème fraîche

Kosher salt and coarsely ground black pepper

FOR THE SALMON

1 whole skin-on side of salmon (about 3½ pounds), pin bones removed (see headnote)

2 tablespoons olive oil

Kosher salt and freshly ground black pepper

5 dill sprigs

1 lemon, very thinly sliced

WHOLE BAKED SIDE OF SALMON WITH HORSERADISH CREAM

1
MAKE THE HORSERADISH CREAM: In a small bowl, whisk together the horseradish, lemon juice, crème fraîche, and salt and pepper to taste. Chill until ready to serve.

2
MAKE THE SALMON: Preheat the oven to 450°F. Line an 18 x 13–inch rimmed sheet pan with parchment paper.

3
Place the salmon, skin-side down, in the center of the prepared sheet pan. Rub the salmon with the olive oil and season generously with salt and pepper. Distribute the dill on top of the salmon and arrange the lemon slices over the top.

4
Roast just until the salmon is opaque but still pink in the center (it's okay to make a small cut and peek!), about 15 minutes. Serve warm or at room temperature with the horseradish cream alongside.

Asparagus and tarragon are a classic combo that is ready for its comeback. When cooking large eggs, you should have set whites and molten yolks at seven minutes. If your eggs are smaller or larger, add or subtract a minute to the cook time accordingly and watch like a hawk to avoid overcooking. Those runny yolks are critical, since they fortify the vinaigrette and make for a richer sauce.

SERVES 6 to 8
SKILL LEVEL 4

ASPARAGUS WITH TARRAGON VINAIGRETTE AND 7-MINUTE EGGS

2 pounds asparagus, trimmed, ends peeled

½ cup lemon-scented extra-virgin olive oil

¼ cup white wine vinegar

2 tablespoons chopped fresh tarragon

1 garlic clove, minced

Kosher salt

5 large eggs

1

Fill a large pot with 1 inch of water, set a steamer basket inside, and bring the water to a boil. Fill a large bowl with ice and water to make an ice bath. Add the asparagus to the steamer basket, cover with the lid, and steam for 3 to 5 minutes, depending on thickness, until the asparagus is just tender but still bright green. Place the asparagus in the ice bath to stop the cooking. Drain and set aside.

2

Put the olive oil, vinegar, tarragon, garlic, and a pinch of salt in a jar. Cover with a lid and shake vigorously. Taste and adjust the seasoning with salt as necessary.

3

Put the asparagus on a plate or platter and drizzle with the dressing; toss to coat. Let marinate in the refrigerator until ready to serve.

4

Bring 4 inches of water to a boil in a medium pot. Fill a large bowl with ice and water to make an ice bath. Using a slotted spoon, gently lower the eggs, one at a time,

RECIPE CONTINUES

into the boiling water in a single layer. Set a timer for 7 minutes.

5

After 7 minutes, drain the eggs and place them in the ice bath until they're cool enough to handle. Peel and set aside.

6

Just before serving, halve the eggs and arrange them on top of the asparagus.

Pro Host
Checklist

The party pro thinks of courtesies and details the amateur doesn't, like:

- Putting a power strip with extra phone chargers in the foyer for drained guests

- Setting out floss, mints, extra hand towels, and matches in the restrooms

- Placing small piles of cocktail napkins where guests will congregate and spill

- Adding lemon wedges and mint sprigs to water carafes

- Chilling a couple bottles of dry champagne or prosecco to offer with dessert and one last toast to new friendships and old

- Prepping a plate of chocolates or truffles to pass just as the evening is about to end

FOR THE MERINGUE

1 cup sugar

1 tablespoon cornstarch

4 large egg whites

Pinch of kosher salt

1 teaspoon vanilla extract

1 teaspoon white vinegar

FOR THE LEMON CURD

½ cup sugar

4 large egg yolks

2 tablespoons grated lemon zest

½ cup fresh lemon juice

½ cup (1 stick) unsalted butter, cubed

TO ASSEMBLE

1 cup heavy cream

2 cups ripe, seasonal fresh fruit like berries, cherries, currants, or even kiwis (pitted and sliced or cut as necessary)

Begin making this airy Pavlova the day before, since the meringue needs to cool in the oven overnight to harden into crispy sweetness. You can also make the curd ahead of time and store it in the fridge, but don't whip the cream and assemble the dessert until the last minute or you'll risk ruining the dance of crackly and soft that ensues when the curd embraces the meringue.

PAVLOVA

1

MAKE THE MERINGUE: Position a rack in lower third of the oven and preheat the oven to 275°F. Line a baking sheet with parchment paper and trace a 9-inch circle onto the paper (you can use a cake pan as a guide). After tracing the circle, flip the parchment over so the ink side is facing the baking sheet.

2

Whisk the sugar and cornstarch together in a small bowl; set aside.

3

In the bowl of a stand mixer fitted with the whisk attachment, beat the egg whites with a pinch of salt on medium speed until they take on air and begin to hold soft peaks. Add the sugar-cornstarch mixture, a few teaspoons at a time, until all of it is incorporated. Increase the speed to high, add the vanilla and vinegar, and beat until glossy stiff peaks form, about 5 minutes more.

4

With a rubber spatula, transfer the meringue into the center of the circle traced on the parchment paper. Working from the center outward, spread the meringue to fill the circle. Bake for 1 hour, then turn the oven off. Crack the oven door open (the handle of a wooden spoon works well for this) and leave the meringue in the oven overnight to cool slowly.

5

MAKE THE LEMON CURD: Make a double boiler by

RECIPE CONTINUES

placing a medium stainless steel bowl on top of a pot filled with 2 inches of water (the bottom of the bowl should not touch the water). Bring the water to a simmer; do not let it boil.

6

Off heat, whisk together the sugar and egg yolks in the bowl until they begin to lighten in color. Add the lemon zest and juice to the mixture and whisk to combine.

7

Place the bowl over the simmering water. Stir the egg yolk mixture continuously with a rubber spatula or wooden spoon until the mixture thickens, 10 to 12 minutes.

8

Remove the bowl from the pot and whisk in the butter cubes, one a time, waiting to add the next until each

is completely incorporated. If you'd like, strain the curd through a fine-mesh sieve to ensure it's completely smooth.

9

Transfer the curd to a nonreactive container (such as stainless steel, ceramic, or glass) and place a layer of plastic wrap directly against the surface of the curd. (This will prevent a skin from forming.) Refrigerate until ready to use.

10

ASSEMBLE THE PAVLOVA: In the bowl of a stand mixer fitted with the whisk attachment, whip the cream until soft peaks form.

11

Just before serving, set the meringue on a serving plate and top it with the curd first, then the whipped cream and fresh fruit.

Friendsgiving

MENU

Friendsgiving is America's favorite foodie holiday minus the familial obligations that make Thanksgiving an annual chafe. Forget the annoying second-cousins-once-removed who fake a gluten allergy because they don't want to eat the stuffing. Free yourself of your dad's insistence that dinner begin promptly at 3 p.m., ensuring that everyone will be sober and hungry again, with nowhere to go, by 8 p.m. Hell, forget the dried-out turkey and lose the cornucopia napkin rings. Friendsgiving is a *Seinfeld*-ian "Festivus" for celebrating your chosen family—the folks who, in the twenty-first century, are just as likely to provide the support, dating advice, and occasional loans as your blood relatives were expected to in ages past.

These recipes all riff on a modern American menu that borrows from the most delicious imported dining trends to cross our tables since we became wise enough to celebrate this made-up holiday. So we swap a whole turkey for hoisin BBQ–glazed turkey breast and the mashed potatoes for sweet potatoes with gremolata. The stuffing becomes a panzanella salad and there's pumpkin in mousse form only. We roast our cranberries, serve Zinfandel because *of course*, and set the table as traditionally or oddly as we like. Because . . . well, we can, and because no one invited your judgy sister and her print magazine ideas about what "Americana" looks like.

So from our friend family to yours, happy Friendsgiving!

Skill Level

Friendsgiving requires the juggling of many dishes at once, so appoint a lieutenant to supervise and attenuate any mishaps. The mousse and turkey need a certain deftness; give those to the most skilled.

Special Equipment

- Microwave

- Stand mixer

- Three 18 x 13–inch baking dishes or rimmed sheet pans

Game Plan

- **The Night Before:** Prepare the cashews and salami

- **Four Hours Before:** Make the mousse

- **Two Hours Before:** Roast the turkey

- **One and a Half Hours Before:** Make the poutine

- **One Hour Before:** Bake the cranberry sauce and make the panzanella

- **45 Minutes Before:** Make the mac 'n' cheese

- **30 Minutes Before:** Make the cheese board and sweet potatoes

Wine Ideas

A lush California Chardonnay and a spicy Oregon Pinot Noir are two fantastic wines for the dinner table. They're similarly textured and versatile with multiple dishes on the table at this turkey-focused meal. (And don't forget the requisite holiday Zinfandel.)

These recipes all riff on a modern American menu that borrows from the most delicious imported dining trends to cross our tables since we became wise enough to celebrate this made-up holiday.

Pro-Tip: Clean-Plate Club

One of the roughest parts of holiday feasting is the cleanup, especially if you dress up the event with cloth napkins and candles. Save yourself some morning-after mess:

- **Line:** Before roasting or baking, line all sheet pans and roasters with aluminum foil or parchment paper for easy cleanup later. When the party's over, you'll have much less scrubbing and scouring to do when you rinse, remove, and recycle that liner.

- **Soak:** Avoid stained linen napkins by soaking them in a bucket of warm, sudsy water as soon as dinner is over. You can hide the bucket in your bathtub (behind the shower curtain) if you don't have a basement or laundry room. The next day, wring them out or run them through the spin cycle before immediately washing.

- **Chill:** Don't use candlesticks on a tableclothed table unless you have holders that will reliably catch the dripping wax (a pain to remove). No candle holders? Buy a bunch of votive candles instead. To remove wax from the inside of the votive the next day, place them on a small sheet pan, fill each votive with cold water, and place in the fridge. The wax will be floating in the water for easy removal about a day later.

(see photograph on pages 160–161)

CRISPY SALAMI AND CASHEW-CRUSTED CASHEWS

SERVES 10
SKILL LEVEL 2

FOR THE CRISPY SALAMI

1 bunch thyme

4 ounces thinly sliced salami

1 tablespoon grated lemon zest (from about 1 lemon)

1 teaspoon Aleppo pepper

FOR THE CASHEW-CRUSTED CASHEWS

24 ounces whole raw cashews

2 tablespoons coriander seeds

2 tablespoons sugar

1 teaspoon cayenne powder

Grated zest of 3 limes

2 egg whites

1

MAKE THE CRISPY SALAMI: Preheat the oven to 350°F. Line a sheet pan with parchment paper.

2

Spread the thyme in one layer on the prepared sheet pan. Top the thyme sprigs with the salami in one layer. Sprinkle the salami with the lemon zest and Aleppo pepper.

3

Bake the salami until its edges darken and appear crispy, 7 to 8 minutes. Remove from the oven and let cool to room temperature. Increase the oven temperature to 400°F.

4

MAKE THE CASHEW-CRUSTED CASHEWS: In a small food processor, combine 8 ounces (about a third) of the cashews, the coriander seeds, sugar, cayenne, and lime zest and pulse into a fine seasoning flour. Pour into a medium bowl and set aside.

5

In a separate bowl, whisk the egg whites until they begin to foam, about 3 minutes. Pour the remaining 16 ounces whole cashews into the egg whites and toss. Pour the cashews into a strainer and let any excess egg white drip off.

6

In a medium bowl, toss one-quarter of the whole cashews with one-quarter of the seasoning powder and place on a sheet pan. Continue with the remaining cashews and powder in three additional batches.

7

Bake the cashews until lightly browned, about 10 minutes.

You're smart to skip the full bird for this turkey breast roasted in a tangy-sweet hoisin sauce. It's faster and easier and doesn't require a brine to ensure juiciness. Just use a meat thermometer to aim for 160°F at the meat's center to guarantee a succulent outcome.

SERVES 10
SKILL LEVEL 3

HOISIN BBQ-GLAZED TURKEY BREAST

1 (8- to 9-pound) bone-in, skin-on, whole turkey breast, at room temperature

½ cup (1 stick) unsalted butter, at room temperature

¾ cup hoisin sauce

2 tablespoons kosher salt

3 tablespoons chile-garlic sauce (such as sambaloelek)

3 tablespoons rice vinegar

2 tablespoons sesame oil

1 teaspoon black sesame seeds

1
Preheat the oven to 425°F. Line a rimmed sheet pan with aluminum foil. Pat the turkey dry with paper towels.

2
In a small bowl, combine the butter and ¼ cup of the hoisin sauce. Rub the hoisin-butter mixture over and under the skin of the turkey. Season the turkey all over with the salt. Transfer the turkey skin-side up to the sheet pan.

3
Roast the turkey for 15 minutes. Reduce the oven temperature to 350°F and roast for 1 hour more.

4
Meanwhile, in a medium saucepan, combine the remaining ½ cup hoisin sauce, the chile-garlic sauce, vinegar, sesame oil, and sesame seeds. Bring to a simmer over medium heat and cook until thickened, 5 to 10 minutes. Remove from the heat.

5
After the 1 hour, brush half the hoisin BBQ sauce onto the turkey. Roast until the internal temperature reaches 160°F, 30 to 45 minutes more. Transfer the turkey to a cutting board, drape with foil, and let rest for 10 to 15 minutes.

6
Using a sharp knife, cut the meat away in a single piece from each side of the breastbone. Then cut the meat crosswise into ½-inch-thick slices. Bring the remaining hoisin BBQ sauce to a boil over high heat. Serve the sliced turkey with the hot hoisin BBQ sauce on the side.

SERVES 10
SKILL LEVEL 3

1 pound cavatappi pasta (or elbows)

4 cups whole milk

2 tablespoons chopped fresh chives

Kosher salt and freshly ground black pepper

1 teaspoon dry mustard

Pinch of cayenne pepper

8 ounces sharp cheddar cheese, shredded

4 ounces mozzarella cheese, shredded

2 ounces cream cheese

1 teaspoon hot sauce

½ cup panko breadcrumbs

2 tablespoons unsalted butter, cut into small pieces

We cook the pasta directly in the milk to save some dishes (Friendsgiving cleanup is enough of a chore) and to create a starchy base for the sauce, which is made right in the same pan. Panko breadcrumbs become a crunchy foil to the creaminess after they broil at the end.

ONE-PAN CHEDDAR MAC 'N' CHEESE

1

Combine the pasta, milk, chives, 1 cup water, 2 teaspoons salt, several grinds of black pepper, the mustard, and the cayenne in a large, high-sided, broiler-safe sauté pan. Bring to a simmer over medium heat and cook, stirring constantly, until the pasta is al dente and the liquid is very starchy, 6 to 8 minutes. Remove from the heat.

2

Add all but ½ cup of the cheddar cheese, the mozzarella, cream cheese, and hot sauce to the skillet. Stir to combine and to melt the cheeses into the sauce.

(You can hold the mac and cheese in the refrigerator at this stage until ready to serve; reheat it over medium heat, thinning it out with a few tablespoons of water as needed, before proceeding.)

3

When ready to serve, preheat the broiler. In a small bowl, combine the breadcrumbs and remaining ½ cup cheddar cheese. Sprinkle the breadcrumb mixture evenly over the mac and cheese and dot with the butter. Broil, watching closely, until golden brown, about 5 minutes.

Pretentious dweebs look down their nose at microwaves. Julia Child loved hers and so does every entertainer who knows that the ends trump the means when there are hungry mouths to feed but limited cooking surfaces. Save yourself some time to savor this dish's spicy, tangy flavors.

MICROWAVED SWEET POTATOES WITH SPICY GINGER-SOY HERB SALAD

4 large or 6 medium sweet potatoes, scrubbed clean

1 teaspoon grated lime zest

3 tablespoons fresh lime juice

1 cup packed fresh cilantro leaves, coarsely chopped

3 scallions, sliced

1 or 2 serrano or Fresno chiles, seeded and thinly sliced lengthwise

1 (2-inch) piece fresh ginger, peeled and julienned

1 garlic clove, grated

2 tablespoons olive oil

1 teaspoon soy sauce

1

Using a fork, prick the sweet potatoes all over. Place up to 4 potatoes in the microwave and microwave on high until fork-tender, about 10 minutes for medium potatoes and 15 minutes for large ones. Remove and repeat with the remaining potatoes as needed. (Alternatively, bake the potatoes on a foil-lined sheet pan in a preheated 425°F oven for 1 to 1½ hours.)

2

In a medium bowl, combine the lime zest and juice, cilantro, scallions, serranos, ginger, garlic, oil, and soy sauce and toss to combine.

3

Halve the potatoes lengthwise down the center. Cut each half lengthwise into 3 pieces. Top the potatoes with the cilantro mixture and serve.

These cranberries are pure Americana, so we roast them to add a whiff of "what's that?" to their sweet finish. Even better: The sauce improves with a bit of rest, so make it ahead and refrigerate overnight. Let it come back to room temp before serving time.

SERVES 10

SKILL LEVEL 1

OVEN-ROASTED CRANBERRY SAUCE

1

Preheat the oven to 350°F.

2

In a parchment paper–lined 18 × 13–inch baking dish or rimmed sheet pan, stir together the cranberries, brown sugar, orange zest and juice, lime zest and juice, star anise, cinnamon stick, ginger, and salt.

3

Bake until the cranberries burst and the sauce has thickened, about 30 minutes. Remove the star anise and cinnamon stick. Serve at room temperature.

24 ounces fresh cranberries

1 cup packed light brown sugar

Zest and juice of 1 orange

Zest and juice of 1 lime

3 star anise pods

1 cinnamon stick

1 (1½-inch) piece fresh ginger, peeled and grated

½ teaspoon kosher salt

4 tablespoons (½ stick) unsalted butter

3 tablespoons olive oil

2 pounds haricots verts or green beans, ends trimmed

Kosher salt and freshly ground black pepper

2 garlic cloves, finely chopped

10 ounces shiitake mushrooms, stems removed, thinly sliced

2 tablespoons all-purpose flour

2 cups vegetable stock

1 cup cheese curds or diced fresh mozzarella cheese

1 cup store-bought french-fried onions

If you call this a green bean casserole, someone's going to get lost in adolescent nostalgia. So call it a poutine and consider this side dish on-trend. We kept the classic canned onions but added gravy and cheese curds with a nod to our northern neighbors.

GREEN BEAN POUTINE

1
Heat 2 tablespoons of the butter and 1 tablespoon of the oil in a large nonstick skillet over medium-high heat. Add the haricots verts, ½ teaspoon salt, and a few grinds of pepper. Cover and cook, stirring occasionally, until the beans are just tender, 8 to 10 minutes. Add the garlic, stir to combine, and cook for 1 minute. Transfer the beans to a gratin dish or platter.

2
In the same skillet, melt 1 tablespoon of the butter and 1 tablespoon of the oil over medium-high heat. Add half the shiitake mushrooms and cook, stirring occasionally, until browned, about 8 minutes. Season with salt and pepper and set aside. Repeat with the remaining mushrooms, butter, and oil.

3
Return all the mushrooms to the pan. Add the flour and cook, stirring constantly, until the flour is light golden, 1 to 2 minutes. Add the stock and cook, stirring constantly, until the gravy is completely incorporated and smooth; simmer until thickened, about 5 minutes more. Season with salt and pepper and remove from the heat.

4
Top the beans with the cheese curds. Pour the hot mushroom gravy over the curds and down the center of the beans, leaving the edges exposed. Finish with the crispy onions and serve immediately.

We've replaced traditional stuffing with a panzanella salad in our Friendsgiving menu, a nod to Italian American eateries everywhere. Let the salad sit for at least 30 minutes before serving.

SERVES 10
SKILL LEVEL 3

PANZANELLA STUFFING SALAD

1

Preheat the oven to 400°F.

2

On a large rimmed sheet pan, toss the focaccia with 2 tablespoons of the olive oil, ½ teaspoon salt, and a few grinds of pepper. Bake until golden, about 10 minutes. Transfer to a large bowl.

3

Heat 2 tablespoons of the oil in a large skillet over medium-high heat. Add the sausage and break it into 1-inch pieces. Cook, stirring occasionally, until well browned, 8 to 10 minutes. Add the wine, bring to a simmer, and cook until almost all the liquid has cooked off. Remove from the heat.

4

Add the sausage mixture, onion, fennel, radicchio, pear, arugula, vinegar, and remaining 2 tablespoons oil to the bowl with the bread. Toss to combine and season to taste with salt and pepper. Let sit for up to 30 minutes so the bread soaks up all the juices.

5

Just before serving, add the basil and toss to combine and redistribute the juices. Add more oil and vinegar, if necessary, to moisten.

3 cups 1-inch-cubed focaccia or baguette

6 tablespoons extra-virgin olive oil, plus more if needed

Kosher salt and freshly ground black pepper

1 pound hot or sweet Italian sausage, casings removed

1 cup dry white wine

1 small red onion, thinly sliced

1 bulb fennel, halved, cored, and thinly sliced crosswise

1 head radicchio, core removed, sliced ½ inch thick

1 red Anjou pear, cored and thinly sliced

5 ounces baby arugula

¼ cup white wine vinegar, plus more if needed

1 cup fresh basil, large leaves torn

This mousse needs to chill twice, so be sure to start this early so it'll be waiting in the fridge for you after dinner! Note: The USDA doesn't recommend consuming raw egg, which this recipe contains.

SERVES 10
SKILL LEVEL 4

1 envelope unflavored powdered gelatin

2 cups canned pumpkin puree

4 large eggs, separated

¼ cup maple syrup

1 teaspoon pumpkin pie spice

1 teaspoon vanilla extract

¼ cup sugar

2 cups chilled heavy cream

2 cups whipped marshmallow topping (preferably Marshmallow Fluff)

1 16-ounce package gingersnaps, finely crushed, with some reserved for garnish

PUMPKIN MOUSSE WITH GINGERSNAPS AND MARSHMALLOW WHIPPED CREAM

1

Put ¼ cup water in a small saucepan (off the heat), and sprinkle the gelatin over. Let soften for 5 minutes. Set the pan over medium heat and heat until the gelatin has dissolved, about 1 minute. Remove from the heat.

2

In a large bowl, combine the pumpkin puree and softened gelatin and stir to combine. Add the egg yolks, maple syrup, pumpkin pie spice, and vanilla; whisk until smooth.

3

In another large bowl or in the bowl of a stand mixer fitted with the whisk attachment, whip the egg whites and sugar to medium peaks. Gently fold the egg whites into the pumpkin mixture.

4

In another large bowl or in the clean mixer bowl, whip 1 cup of the heavy cream to medium peaks; gently fold the whipped cream into pumpkin mixture.

5

Cover and refrigerate until chilled, at least 30 minutes.

6

In another large bowl or in the mixer bowl, whip the remaining 1 cup heavy cream to medium peaks.

RECIPE CONTINUES

Add the marshmallow topping and whisk until completely smooth.

7

In individual serving cups, such as mugs or short water glasses, add one layer of the pumpkin mousse. Top with one layer of gingersnap crumbs. Top with another layer of the pumpkin mousse, followed by a layer of gingersnap crumbs. Top with the marshmallow whipped cream. Sprinkle the remaining ginger snaps over the top of each individual mousse to garnish. Chill for 30 minutes or until ready to serve.

Last-Minute Checklist

By the time the guests are about to arrive, you might be running out of the brain cells needed to tend to details.

So, once the bar is set for first arrivers, do this:

- Light the candles and dim the lights.

- Start the playlist.

- Empty all smelly trash cans and run the dishwasher.

- Adjust the thermostat to prep for all the body heat about to arrive.

- Fill your laundry basket with any random clothes, papers, laptops, and other unorganized essentials still lying around, then hide the basket.

- Brush your teeth, fix your hair, layer some scents (no time to shower!), and slip on your practical (read: black or navy) hosting getup.

- Spritz a generous wad of paper towels with glass cleaner and give all your bathroom surfaces a quick shine.

- Pour yourself a drink, smile broadly at your accomplishment, and put on a casual air that suggests "What? All this? Why, it's nothing at all."

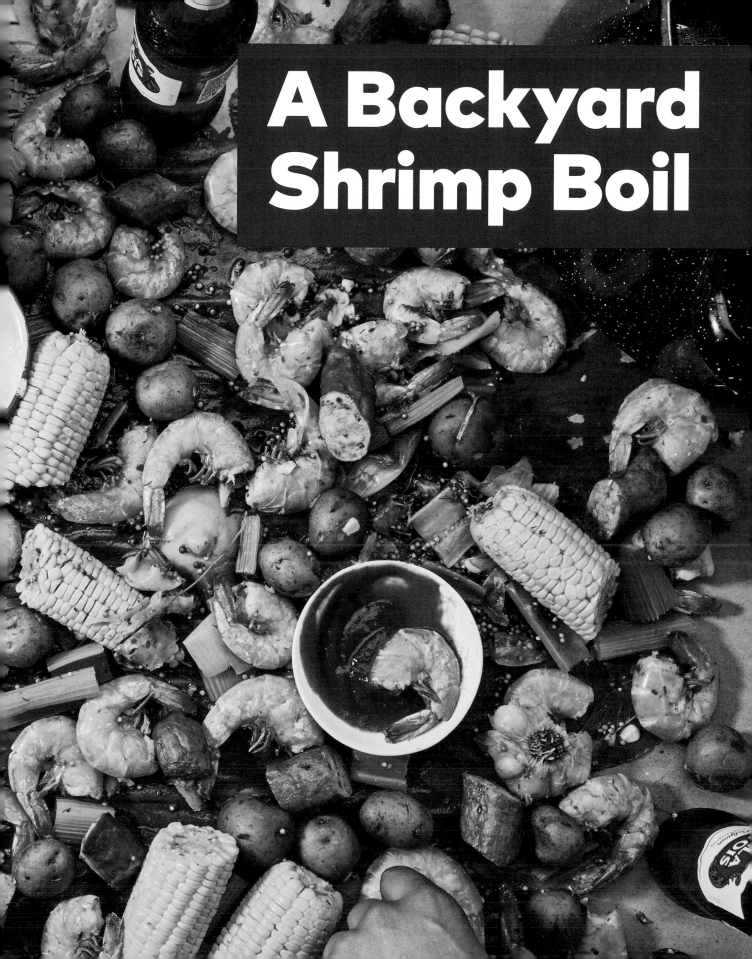

A Backyard Shrimp Boil

MENU

Sure, this menu would be a winner for any long weekend between May and September. But if you want to be a summer superhero, invite friends for this backyard shrimp boil in the dead of August just as the season starts to annoy. Gather your crankiest neighbors and everyone else who failed to schedule a hot-weather getaway and offer them this afternoon antidote to their sweaty workday commutes and bland beach-body diets.

Everyone will appreciate a delicious distraction, but you're trying to relax, too. So this menu features a buffet, perfect for an accordioning guest list of who-knows-how-many-will-show. And you'll serve outside, of course, for quick cleanup: Lawns don't stain.

Serve ice-cold spiked tea-and-lemonade Palmers to give your guests a caffeinated lift while they ease into the party. Spicy watermelon is spiked, too: *literally* (on skewers) and, if you like, *figuratively* with tequila for simple, buzzy snacking without a shot glass. There's a soft-yet-crunchy salad of stone fruit and jicama just as peaches peak. And the main attraction is a messy, finger-licking shrimp boil with cheesy biscuits that will make everyone feel like a kid. By the time you roll out the strawberry pie, temperatures will have cooled and autumn's arrival won't be so welcome after all.

Skill Level

If anyone in your party has a soft touch, let them make the biscuits; the gentler the kneading the better. The shrimp is prep intensive, so employ two or three hardy souls to plow through it.

Special Equipment

- Large pot (like a lobster pot)

- 9-inch pie tin

- Stand mixer

- 8-inch bamboo skewers

- Two 18 x 13-inch rimmed sheet pans

Game Plan

- **The Night Before:** Make the pie

- **Four Hours Before:** Prep the skewers

- **One and a Half Hours Before:** Make the biscuits

- **One Hour Before:** Make the shrimp

- **45 Minutes Before:** Make the Palmers

- **30 Minutes Before:** Make the salad

- **Right Before Serving:** Finish the skewers

Wine Ideas

A fruity and fresh Spanish Rueda is a fun way to play outside with summer fare. A red Rioja Crianza will have enough freshness and oomph to handle the shrimp boil with sausage.

Serve ice-cold spiked tea-and-lemonade Palmers to give your guests a caffeinated lift while they ease into the party.

Pro-Tip: Creating Atmosphere (Literally)

When you're hosting more than a handful of friends in warmer months, *consider your air-conditioning situation before planning.* If you're entertaining outdoors, no problem: People who can't stand the heat will get the heck out of your kitchen, where you wanted space to prep anyway. But if you're hosting in a smaller apartment or one where the A/C is weak, drop the thermostat several hours early to pre-cool the place, or plan a different menu where most of the food can be cooked before guests arrive, then finished, quickly on the stove or flashed in the oven just before serving.

Don't mind a hot kitchen: People who can't stand the heat will get the heck out of your kitchen where you wanted space to prep anyway.

This cocktail is half iced tea, half lemonade, and all summer buzz. Be careful with the serving size, because these go down very easily. The longer you let the vodka infuse with the tea, the stronger the flavor, but don't let it go for more than a couple hours or you'll risk bitterness.

SPIKED PALMERS

MAKES 12 to 14 cocktails
SKILL LEVEL 3

FOR THE INFUSED VODKA

4 bags Earl Grey tea

1 (750-milliliter) bottle vodka

FOR THE COCKTAILS

1 cup fresh mint leaves

1 cup Sugar In The Raw

6 Meyer lemons, peeled, quartered, and seeded

Ice

Meyer lemon wheels, for garnish

1

MAKE THE EARL GREY VODKA: Add the tea bags to the bottle of vodka. Allow to steep for at least 1 to 2 hours, but no longer than 2 hours.

2

MAKE THE COCKTAILS: Combine 2½ cups of the infused vodka, 1½ cups water, the mint, sugar, and lemon quarters in a blender. Blend without ice until well combined. Strain through a fine-mesh sieve into a glass pitcher. Serve over lots of ice and garnish each drink with a Meyer lemon wheel.

For an extra punch, drizzle two shots of blanco tequila on the finished skewers. Go slow with the chile powder: A little bit goes a long way.

SERVES 6 to 8
SKILL LEVEL 1

SPICY WATERMELON SKEWERS

1 small (7- to 8-pound) seedless watermelon

Zest and juice of 1 lime

2 tablespoons kosher salt

1 tablespoon ancho chile powder

1

Remove the rind from the watermelon. Cut the flesh of the melon into 4-inch batons. Thread each baton onto a skewer.

2

Squeeze the lime juice over the batons. Combine the lime zest, salt, and chile powder in a small bowl. Sprinkle over the skewered melon right before serving.

It's easy to screw up a biscuit, especially when you're distracted by many moving pieces in a menu. That's why this recipe has an insurance policy against a failed puck: two kinds of cheese in the batter to keep the texture springy. You can't miss.

SERVES 6 to 8
SKILL LEVEL 4

CHEESY BISCUITS

FOR THE BISCUITS

1 cup (2 sticks) cold unsalted butter, cubed, plus more for greasing

4 cups all-purpose flour, plus more as needed

3 tablespoons baking powder

2 teaspoons baking soda

¼ teaspoon kosher salt

2½ cups grated sharp cheddar cheese

1 cup chopped scallions

½ cup grated Parmesan cheese

1¾ cups low-fat buttermilk

FOR THE TOPPING

⅓ cup unsalted butter

1 tablespoon Old Bay seasoning

1

MAKE THE BISCUITS: Preheat the oven to 450°F. Line two 18 x 13–inch sheet pans with parchment paper and grease them with butter.

2

Whisk together the flour, baking powder, baking soda, and salt in a bowl. Stir in the cheddar, scallions, and Parmesan.

3

Add the cold butter and work it into the flour mixture with your fingers, coating the cubes with flour and pinching each one to flatten (make a snapping motion with your thumb and first two fingers).

4

Add the buttermilk to the dry mix and stir with a fork (you can hold the fork stationary while spinning the bowl with your other hand) until a loose, shaggy dough begins to come together. Using a spoon, drop the biscuit dough in ¼-cup-ish dollops onto the prepared pans, keeping them evenly spaced apart. Bake until light golden brown, 15 to 18 minutes.

5

MEANWHILE, MAKE THE TOPPING: Melt the butter and Old Bay in a small saucepan over medium heat. Brush, pour, or dab the butter topping on the biscuits and serve.

A shrimp boil is best served outdoors, where all the mess can be washed away with a hose later. If that's not possible, be warned that this is an interactive entrée meant to be eaten by hand. Spread out a nice checkered plastic tablecloth to protect your table, then layer clean newspaper on top. Why bother? Because nothing smacks of summer quite like a shrimp boil. Note: If you don't have a large enough pot for the boil, two smaller pots will work.

SHRIMP BOIL WITH SAUSAGE

1

Combine the celery, onions, garlic, lemons, salt, bay leaves, thyme, coriander seeds, dill seeds, mustard seeds, red pepper flakes, cayenne, allspice, peppercorns, paprika, cloves, and 2 gallons water in one very large pot (like a lobster pot) and bring to a boil. Reduce the heat to medium and simmer, stirring occasionally, until the onions and celery are soft and the flavors have melded, about 40 minutes.

2

Add the potatoes to the broth and cook until almost tender, about 15 minutes. Add the corn and cook for another 6 minutes. Add the shrimp and sausage and cook, stirring occasionally, until the shrimp are just cooked through, about 4 minutes more.

3

Using a large slotted spoon, transfer the shrimp, sausage, corn, and potatoes to a large paper-lined table or other surface. Serve with bowls of melted butter, lemon wedges, and the reserved cooking liquid.

6 celery stalks, coarsely chopped

2 yellow onions, quartered

2 heads garlic, halved crosswise

2 lemons, halved

1 cup kosher salt

5 bay leaves

3 sprigs thyme

3 tablespoons coriander seeds

2 tablespoons dill seeds

2 tablespoons mustard seeds

1½ tablespoons red pepper flakes

1½ tablespoons cayenne pepper

1 tablespoon whole allspice berries

1 tablespoon whole black peppercorns

1 tablespoon sweet paprika

8 whole cloves

3 pounds small red potatoes

6 ears of corn, cut in half crosswise

5 pounds large shrimp, unpeeled

1 pound smoked sausage, cut into 1-inch pieces

Melted butter, for serving

Lemon wedges, for serving

4 pounds peaches

Kosher salt

1 large or 2 medium jicamas (about 30 ounces)

2 tablespoons sherry vinegar

2 tablespoons extra-virgin olive oil

Coarsely ground black pepper

2 cups fresh basil leaves

Ripe summer peaches play nicely with crisp matchstick jicama in this unexpected salad. In fact, the combo is so successful that even defrosted frozen peaches will work, if you're making the recipe out of season. Really.

PEACH, BASIL, AND JICAMA SALAD

1

Halve, pit, and slice the peaches into 1-inch wedges. Place in a bowl and season liberally with salt.

2

Peel and cut the jicama into thick matchsticks, about 1/3 inch thick. Add to the bowl along with the sherry vinegar, olive oil, and pepper. Toss to coat, then refrigerate until ready to serve.

3

Just before serving, tear the basil into the bowl and toss.

You're *supposed* to "shingle" the strawberries carefully around the pie, as Martha would do. But you're not Martha and those Spiked Palmers are strong, so don't hesitate to just spoon the berries into a creatively chaotic mound if you're not feeling meticulous today.

STRAWBERRY PIE

FOR THE CRUST

1 sleeve saltines

½ cup (1 stick) unsalted butter, at room temperature

2 tablespoons granulated sugar

FOR THE FILLING

1 (8-ounce) package cream cheese, at room temperature

½ cup powdered sugar

¼ teaspoon grated lemon zest

½ teaspoon fresh lemon juice

1 cup chilled heavy cream

1 pound strawberries, hulled and sliced

¼ cup granulated sugar

Kosher salt

1

MAKE THE CRUST: Preheat the oven to 350°F.

2

Put the saltines into a food processor and pulse until pulverized. Combine the cracker crumbs, butter, and granulated sugar in a bowl and knead into a dough with your fingers. Press into a 9-inch pie plate and refrigerate for 15 minutes.

3

Bake until lightly browned, about 20 minutes. Chill for 15 minutes.

4

MAKE THE FILLING: In a bowl, beat together the cream cheese, powdered sugar, lemon zest, and lemon juice.

5

In a large bowl or the bowl of a stand mixer fitted with the whisk attachment, whip the cream to stiff peaks. Fold the whipped cream into the cream cheese mixture.

6

Toss the strawberries with the granulated sugar and a pinch of salt in a medium bowl. Let sit for 15 minutes to allow the salt and sugar to draw juices from the berries.

7

Drain the strawberries, reserving the liquid. Cook the liquid in a small pot over medium heat until syrupy, about 10 minutes. Let cool. Add the strawberries to the cooled syrup.

8

Spread the cream cheese mixture over the crust and smooth the top. Top with strawberries and their syrup. Chill until serving.

A Vegetarian Dinner for Omnivores

MENU

Serving a vegetarian dinner to meat-lovers isn't the statement it once was. These days, the humble vegetable has moved to the center of the plate, propelled by modern attitudes about wellness, animal welfare, the environment, and wallets (meat is expensive!).

But you can reserve the social studies for dinner party patter, because serving a meatless meal to proud carnivores is simply a fun challenge. It requires culinary creativity and above-average cooking skills, since each vegetable will have to shine a little brighter to be a star. And the stakes will be raised knowing that someone's bacon-obsessed boyfriend will be looking for a reason to text *"I'm still hungry"* across the table. He's tedious for sure, but you appreciate a challenging opponent.

No fears. You'll disarm eye-rollers with delicious sophistication by balancing and mirroring spice profiles and textures not only *within* each dish but *among* them. So briny veggies appear in a cucumber martini at the start and again in a crispy rice bowl, this time *tea pickled*—all the while providing a crunchy foil to the bowl's soft egg. Earthy mushroom "chips" in one dish duel with airy miso-lime dressing in another. And the spices on those mushrooms will be remembered when guests taste the tang of a different dish, the Broccolini and parsnips, later. This is a foodie's show-off affair where pretension will be forgiven for deliciousness. Haters gonna hate, but tonight even the butcher's daughter will swoon.

Skill Level

The crispy rice here delivers big time, but needs a little time and artistry. The rest is simple.

Special Equipment

- 12-inch cast-iron skillet

- 8-inch square baking dish

- Two 18 x 13–inch rimmed sheet pans

Because serving a meatless meal to proud carnivores is simply a fun challenge.

Game Plan

- **Two Days in Advance (Optional):** Prepare the rice

- **The Night Before:** Make the granita

- **Four Hours Before:** Start the slaw and the pickled vegetables

- **Three Hours Before:** Prepare the edamame

- **One Hour Before:** Roast the Broccolini and shiitakes at the same time

- **45 Minutes Before:** Finish the rice

- **30 Minutes Before:** Make the martinis

- **Right Before Serving:** Finish the slaw

Wine Ideas

A crisp Finger Lakes dry Riesling will have enough snap for the veggies on the table. For red, serve a bright, youthful Cru Beaujolais that's dry and lightly fruit-driven with the array of vegetables.

MAKES 8 to 10 cocktails

SKILL LEVEL 3

1 medium cucumber, coarsely chopped

3 cups good-quality gin (like Hendricks or Greenhook)

⅓ cup Cocchi Americano or another dry vermouth

Ice

Skewered pickled vegetables (store-bought or homemade) like green beans or carrots, green olives (like Castelvetrano), and cherry tomatoes or any pretty vegetables, for garnish

The martini gets a refreshing twist in this "pickled" cocktail. Like most martinis, ours is strong, so warn any lightweights on your guest list. If you have room, chill the glasses in the freezer for a frosty effect. For the garnish, create cute little skewers of fresh and pickled vegetables or set up a DIY station for guests to make their own.

CUCUMBER MARTINI WITH PICKLED VEGETABLES

1
Put the chopped cucumber in a food processor and briefly pulse until chunky and juicy (or use a mortar and pestle to roughly muddle the cucumber to the same consistency).

2
Pour the gin and vermouth into a quart container, then add the cucumber with its juice from the food processor. Seal the container and shake vigorously, then allow the mixture to sit for at least 20 minutes before straining through a fine-mesh sieve into a large carafe.

3
Set up a shaker with ice next to the carafe, and when serving, stir the cocktail with ice until it is ice-cold before straining into martini glasses.

4
Garnish with a skewer of the pickled veg and cherry tomatoes and serve.

Edamame makes a great appetizer when the guests don't know each other well. They might be slightly nervous, so giving them something to do with their hands until those first cocktails set in—like separating edamame seeds from their shells as they eat—is simply thoughtful hosting on your part. And the scent of the orange and chili mingling is more welcoming than potpourri any day.

SERVES 4
SKILL LEVEL 1

WARM ORANGE-CHILE EDAMAME

1 orange

3 tablespoons olive oil

1 teaspoon fennel seeds, lightly crushed

4 dried chiles de àrbol

Kosher salt

1 pound frozen edamame in their pods, thawed

3 tablespoons unseasoned rice vinegar

1 tablespoon furikake (Japanese seasoning)

Maldon salt

1

Using a vegetable peeler, remove two 3-inch strips of zest from the orange.

2

Heat a large skillet over medium-high heat and add the olive oil, orange zest, crushed fennel seeds, dried chiles, and 1 teaspoon kosher salt. Cook, stirring occasionally, until the flavors mingle, about 5 minutes. Add the edamame and cook until just tender.

(This step can be done up to 3 hours in advance and the edamame kept at room temperature; reheat before serving.)

3

Add the rice vinegar and toss to combine. Transfer to a serving dish (or serve straight from the pot). Sprinkle with the furikake and a generous pinch of Maldon salt and serve.

1 pound large shiitake mushrooms (caps approximately 4 to 5 inches in diameter), stems removed

3 tablespoons olive oil

1 teaspoon Chinese five-spice powder

Kosher salt and freshly ground black pepper

¼ cup mayonnaise

2 tablespoons white miso paste

1 tablespoon fresh lime juice

½ teaspoon sesame oil

1 or 2 scallions, thinly sliced on an angle

These chips know that it's tough to look good in a dark brown suit. That's why they don't rely on their looks: They've got earthy personality and five-spice zip to help them stand out in a crowded menu. They turn heads every time.

CRISPY FIVE-SPICE SHIITAKE MUSHROOM CHIPS WITH MISO-MAYO SAUCE

1
Preheat the oven to 450°F.

2
Place the shiitake caps on a rimmed sheet pan and drizzle with the olive oil. Massage the olive oil into the mushrooms with your hands to evenly distribute, season with the five-spice powder, salt, and pepper, and toss to coat.

3
Transfer to the oven and roast until the mushrooms are browned and crispy but still tender in the center, flipping them after 30 minutes, about 45 minutes total.

4
Meanwhile, in a small bowl, whisk together the mayo, white miso, and lime juice. Garnish the sauce with the sesame oil and scallions.

5
Serve the chips warm or at room temperature, seasoned to taste with additional salt and pepper, if desired, with the sauce on the side.

You may be wondering if we've lost our minds, including so many spicy notes in a single menu. But you're forgetting that every kind of "hot" is different, and no two chiles kick the same. These recipes take your guests on a wild spice ride, with sharp, dull, fast, slow, and even lingering heats making appearances. These Broccolini like their hot sharp and fast.

SERVES 4
SKILL LEVEL 3

SPICY BROCCOLINI WITH PARSNIPS, SESAME SEEDS, AND CHILE-GARLIC OIL

2 tablespoons sesame seeds

¼ cup olive oil

2 garlic cloves, grated

1¼ teaspoons red pepper flakes

Kosher salt

1¼ pounds parsnips, peeled and cut into 1-inch pieces

2 bunches Broccolini (about 1 pound), ends trimmed, halved lengthwise if large

Juice of ½ lemon

1

Preheat the oven to 450°F.

2

Place the sesame seeds in a small skillet over medium heat. Toast, shaking the pan occasionally, until fragrant and golden, about 5 minutes. Set aside on a small plate.

3

In a small bowl, stir together the olive oil, garlic, red pepper flakes, and 1 teaspoon salt. Reserve 1 tablespoon and add the remainder to a large bowl with the parsnips and Broccolini and toss to coat thoroughly. Place the parsnips on a rimmed sheet pan and transfer to the oven. Roast until softened and beginning to char in places, about 10 minutes. Add Broccolini and roast, flipping once, until all the vegetables are charred and crispy, about 20 minutes more. Remove from the oven, top with the sesame seeds and remaining chile oil, and squeeze the lemon juice on top. Season to taste with additional salt, toss to coat, and serve.

This salad of raw Brussels sprouts with miso and peanuts makes a delicious demonstration of the menu's point that there are countless ways to serve most vegetables. Don't be shy when adding the dressing: The finely shredded sprouts are a dressing sponge.

2 tablespoons white miso paste

2 tablespoons rice vinegar

Zest of ½ lime

1 tablespoon fresh lime juice

1½ teaspoons honey

2 teaspoons grated fresh ginger (from one 2-inch piece)

2 teaspoons sesame oil

3 tablespoons olive oil

Kosher salt and freshly ground black pepper

¾ pound Brussels sprouts, trimmed and thinly sliced lengthwise on a mandoline (3 cups shaved)

1 bunch watercress (about 4 ounces), ends trimmed

3 tablespoons chopped toasted peanuts

BRUSSELS SPROUT SLAW WITH MISO-LIME DRESSING, WATERCRESS, AND PEANUTS

1

In a large bowl, combine the miso, 1 tablespoon of the rice vinegar, the lime zest and juice, honey, ginger, sesame oil, and 2 table-spoons of the olive oil. Whisk until smooth and season to taste with salt and pepper. Add the Brussels sprouts, toss to combine, and transfer to the refrigerator. Let sit for at least 30 minutes or up to 4 hours.

2

Whisk the remaining 1 tablespoon olive oil and 1 tablespoon rice vinegar in a small bowl. Season with salt and pepper. Place the watercress on a serving platter, drizzle with the vinaigrette, and season with salt and pepper. Toss gently with your hands to combine. Top with the Brussels sprouts and peanuts and serve.

The quick-pickling technique in this recipe is easy and flexible: Swap in alt-veggies, like cucumbers, radishes, or even jalapeños, if you're feeling creative.

EXTRA-CRISPY BROWN RICE BOWL WITH TEA-PICKLED VEGETABLES AND SOFT EGGS

2 cups short-grain brown rice

Kosher salt

2 medium carrots, shaved lengthwise with a mandoline or vegetable peeler

1 small turnip, quartered and thinly sliced

1 black tea bag

¾ cup distilled white vinegar

1 tablespoon honey

2 large eggs

3 tablespoons olive oil

4 large shallots, finely chopped

4 garlic cloves, finely chopped

1 tablespoon finely chopped fresh ginger

½ teaspoon red pepper flakes, plus more for serving

6 heads baby bok choy (about 12 ounces), thinly sliced crosswise

½ cup fresh cilantro leaves

½ cup fresh mint leaves

Maldon salt

1

In a medium pot, bring 3½ cups water to a boil over high heat. Add the rice and 2 teaspoons kosher salt, stir, and reduce the heat to maintain a simmer. Cover and cook until the rice is nearly cooked through but still quite toothsome, 35 to 40 minutes. Remove the cover, increase the heat to high, and cook, stirring, until all the moisture has evaporated and the rice begins to stick to the bottom of the pan. Transfer to a paper towel–lined plate and let cool slightly. Transfer to the refrigerator until cold, at least 1 hour or up to 2 days. The drier your rice, the crispier it will be.

2

Meanwhile, place the carrots, turnips, and tea bag in a medium bowl. Combine the vinegar, ½ cup water, the honey, and 2½ teaspoons kosher salt in a medium pot and place over high heat. Bring to a boil, stirring to dissolve the salt. Pour over the vegetables and stir, dunking the tea bag to encourage steeping. If necessary, top with a small plate to ensure the vegetables are covered by the brine. Let sit for at least 1 hour, then remove the tea bag. Keep covered in the refrigerator. Make up to 1 week in advance.

RECIPE CONTINUES

3

Bring a small pot of water to a boil over high heat. Gently lower the eggs into the water, reduce the heat to maintain a simmer, and cook for 7 minutes. Drain and transfer to a small bowl of ice water until chilled. Peel and set aside.

4

When ready to serve, heat a 12-inch cast-iron skillet over high heat until smoking. Add the olive oil, swirl to coat, add the rice, and season with kosher salt. Toss to coat the grains in oil and cook, undisturbed, for 5 minutes. Stir, and cook again, without stirring, for an additional 5 to 6 minutes, until the rice is deeply golden and very crispy. Reduce the heat to medium-high and add the shallots, garlic, ginger, and red pepper flakes. Season with kosher salt and sauté until aromatic, about 3 minutes. Add the bok choy and cook, stirring, until slightly wilted, an additional 3 minutes.

5

Drain the pickled vegetables, reserving the pickling liquid for serving. Halve the soft-boiled eggs. Remove the skillet from the heat and add the pickled vegetables to the center, along with the eggs, cilantro, and mint. Season with Maldon salt, additional red pepper flakes, and a few spoonfuls of the reserved pickling liquid.

How to Make Any Menu
Veggie Friendly

Even if you send out a dozen reminder emails asking guests to let you know in advance about their dietary restrictions, some rude ninny is going to announce minutes before dinner is served that they forgot to mention they're gluten-free/paleo/vegetarian/vegan/flexitarian/following a fad diet/"allergic" to your main dish. Technically, you could frown apologetically and say, "Sorry to hear that."

But you're a superstar host, so you planned for the possibility. When ordering your groceries, always add ingredients for a simple but lovely last-minute salad, like pre-washed salad greens, crumbled Gorgonzola, walnuts, and chives.

Your guest will have to eat whatever they can from your menu, but you can quickly dress the special salad before the main course. Serve it to your special guest, piled high, entrée-style, in a shallow bowl along with a small plate of bread, classy crackers, or crisps.

No last-minute special guests announce themselves tonight? Even better: Your lunch for tomorrow is set.

SERVES 4

SKILL LEVEL 3

1 (13.5-ounce) can light
coconut milk

1¾ cups high-quality
coconut water

8 ounces frozen mango
chunks (about 1½ heaping
cups), or flesh from 1 ripe
mango

Zest and juice of 1 lime, plus
additional zest for serving

2 tablespoons honey, plus
more for garnish

Kosher salt

This light but creamy granita requires extra time in the freezer
to achieve a flaky, frosty texture, so plan accordingly (or make
this the night before).

COCONUT AND MANGO GRANITA WITH LIME AND HONEY

1

In a blender, combine the
coconut milk, coconut water,
mango, lime zest and juice,
honey, and a pinch of salt.
Blend until smooth.

2

Pour into an 8-inch square
baking dish and transfer
to the freezer. Freeze,
stirring (and eventually
scraping) with a fork every
45 minutes, until crystals
form and the mixture is
frozen throughout.

3

When ready to serve, scrape
the granita with a fork
and serve in small dishes.
Garnish with additional
lime zest and a drizzle of
honey.

A Meal for Making Friends

MENU

Turn to this classy but not showy menu when you'd like to get to know a few new faces over the course of an evening. Like when your best friend announces her engagement to a guy you barely know, or when new neighbors move in and you want to get the scoop. Big dinners dilute your focus among many guests, so tonight's dinner is a concentration game—of flavors and attention.

Because cooking with *new* friends makes it easy to figure out how fun someone is . . . or what they're all about. Will they bring an unoaked Chardonnay to pair with the grilled chicken thighs (so sophisticated yet approachable!)? Can they decipher the spiralizer while sharing enticing hearsay from down the hall (you knew you'd like them!)? Do they know if the fork goes on the left or the right? Do they get that it doesn't matter?

By the time you pass the broiled pineapple quarters and offer a round of espresso, all will have been revealed and a return invitation will be in the offing. Or it won't, if they're boring. But who cares: There's leftover yogurt flatbread in the kitchen.

Skill Level

The flatbreads are best prepared as a group—they're fun and creative, and you can't have too many of them.

Special Equipment

- Spiralizer

- Outdoor grill or grill pan

- Three 18 x 13-inch rimmed sheet pans

- 12-inch cast-iron skillet

Game Plan

- **The Night Before:** Season the chicken

- **Four Hours Before:** Make the olives

- **Three Hours Before:** Prepare the flatbread

- **One Hour Before:** Prepare the chicken

- **45 Minutes Before:** Make the beets and potato salad

- **30 Minutes Before:** Make the margaritas

- **Right Before Serving:** Make the pineapple

Turn to this classy but not showy menu when you'd like to get to know a few new faces over the course of an evening.

Wine Ideas

Keep this menu simple with a crowd-pleasing Sancerre sauvignon blanc that's lean and crisp. For the main course, consider a fresh Sicilian red made from Frapatto or Nerello Mascalese.

MAKES 8 cocktails
SKILL LEVEL 2

Smoked salt

Lime wedge, for rimming the glasses

1 medium jalapeño, coarsely chopped

½ cup Cointreau

2 cups reposado tequila

1 cup blood orange juice (fresh or bottled)

¾ cup fresh lime juice

Ice

Meet the classic margarita's sexier, more luscious cousin. Note that all jalapeños are not created equal. Start by muddling one-quarter of a jalapeño first, then taste once you've mixed the ingredients. You can always add more spice, but you can't take it away.

BLOOD ORANGE SPICY MARGARITAS

1
Spread a couple of tablespoons of smoked salt over a small plate. Prepare four glasses by rubbing a lime wedge along the top of each one and rolling the glass in the smoked salt to coat the rim. Set the glasses aside.

2
In a cocktail shaker, muddle one-quarter of the jalapeño until juices are visible.

3
Add the Cointreau to the shaker and swirl around briefly to mix, then empty the contents of the shaker into a pitcher. Add the tequila, blood orange juice, and lime juice and stir with a large spoon.

4
Taste the cocktail and if more spice is desired, muddle additional jalapeño (one-quarter at a time) and add it to mixture, tasting each time before adding more.

5
Strain the cocktail through a fine-mesh sieve into a large carafe for serving, making sure all the seeds are removed.

6
Before serving, chill each cocktail in an ice-filled shaker. Strain over ice into the prepared glasses.

These olives taste best if they have some time to chill out and mingle a bit, so make them hours in advance, if possible, and store them tightly covered. In fact, you can make them up to a week in advance and store them in your fridge until the day before, when you can bring them back to room temp before serving.

SERVES 4

SKILL LEVEL 2

BAR OLIVES WITH LEMON PEEL, BAY LEAVES, AND FRESH CHILES

¾ cup olive oil

Zest of 1 lemon, peeled into strips with a vegetable peeler

1 red cayenne pepper, sliced lengthwise

1 fresh bay leaf

1 teaspoon cumin seeds

2 cups mixed olives (with pits)

Kosher salt and freshly ground black pepper

1

In a medium saucepan, combine the olive oil, lemon zest strips, cayenne pepper, bay leaf, and cumin seeds and cook over low heat, swirling occasionally, until the oil is very fragrant, 4 to 5 minutes.

2

Remove from the heat and add the olives to the warm oil. Allow to sit for at least 10 minutes before serving. Season lightly with salt and black pepper.

2 tablespoons fresh
orange juice

1 tablespoon white wine
vinegar

1 teaspoon Dijon mustard

1 small shallot, minced

¼ cup olive oil

Kosher salt and freshly
ground black pepper

2 medium red beets (about
8 ounces), peeled and
spiralized

2 medium golden beets
(about 8 ounces), peeled and
spiralized

¼ cup fresh mint leaves

¼ cup fresh parsley leaves

2 ounces ricotta salata cheese,
crumbled, for garnish

¼ cup pistachios, toasted and
coarsely chopped, for garnish

If you don't have a spiralizer or if you want to save some time, you can buy pre-spiralized beets at most modern grocers, thanks to the rate at which food fads are making their way to the "prepared veg" aisle. Your Instagram-obsessed friends will busy themselves snapping this gorgeous dish, but rest assured that it tastes as good as it looks, unlike most Insta-fads.

SPIRALIZED BEET SALAD

1

In a small bowl, whisk together the orange juice, vinegar, Dijon, and shallot. Slowly whisk in the olive oil until smooth. Season with salt and pepper.

2

Place the red beets in one medium bowl and the golden beets in another. Toss each with half of the dressing and let marinate for at least 30 minutes. Divide the mint and parsley leaves between the bowls and toss to incorporate. Transfer to a platter, layering the red and golden beet mixtures together. Garnish with the crumbled ricotta salata and chopped pistachios, and serve.

These thighs are equally terrific prepared on a grill pan or an outdoor grill. If cooking outside, you can heat the cast iron directly on the hot grill grates for charring the jalapeños and garlic for the sauce.

GRILLED CHICKEN THIGHS WITH GREEN SAUCE

FOR THE CHICKEN

2 teaspoons coriander seeds

1 teaspoon fennel seeds

1 teaspoon red pepper flakes

½ teaspoon ground cinnamon

Kosher salt

8 bone-in, skin-on chicken thighs (about 2½ pounds total)

FOR THE GREEN SAUCE

4 jalapeños (about 4 ounces)

4 garlic cloves, unpeeled

2 cups packed fresh cilantro leaves and stems

1 teaspoon ground cumin

¼ cup plus 2 tablespoons extra-virgin olive oil, plus more for the grill

1 teaspoon white wine vinegar

Kosher salt and freshly ground black pepper

1

SEASON THE CHICKEN: Combine the coriander seeds, fennel seeds, red pepper flakes, and cinnamon in a spice grinder or mortar and pestle and grind until fully blended. Mix the spice mixture with 4 teaspoons salt in a small bowl.

2

Season the chicken thighs heavily with the spiced salt and refrigerate until ready to cook, up to 24 hours.

3

MAKE THE GREEN SAUCE: Char the jalapeños and garlic in a dry cast-iron skillet over medium-high heat, shaking the pan occasionally, until blackened in spots, about 10 minutes. Remove the stems of the jalapeños and peel the garlic.

Combine the jalapeños, garlic, cilantro, cumin, olive oil, and vinegar in a food processor and pulse just until a chunky paste forms, adding a few tablespoons of water if necessary to loosen it up. Do not overprocess or the herbs will bruise. Season with salt and black pepper and set aside.

4

GRILL THE CHICKEN: If using a grill, prepare the grill and lightly grease the grates with oil. Add the chicken skin-side down. Cook for 5 minutes, until the skin is golden, charred, and crispy, then flip and cook for 3 minutes longer. Cover and cook for about 10 minutes, or until just cooked through and a meat thermometer inserted into the thickest part of the

RECIPE CONTINUES

largest thigh registers 165°F. If using a grill pan, preheat the oven to 425°F. Heat the grill pan over medium-high heat. Lightly grease the pan with oil. In batches, place the chicken thighs in the pan, skin-side down. Cook for 5 minutes, or until the skin is golden, charred, and crispy, then flip and cook for 3 minutes longer. Transfer the thighs to a sheet pan. Continue browning the thighs and adding them to the sheet pan. Place the sheet pan in the oven and bake for about 10 minutes, or until just cooked through and a meat thermometer inserted into the thickest part of the largest thigh registers 165°F.

5

Transfer the cooked chicken to a platter and serve immediately, accompanied by the green sauce and additional cilantro.

How to
Crowdsource a Toast

If you're hosting a party to celebrate someone's birthday, anniversary, or recent accomplishment, you're a great friend. But your duty isn't over once the guests arrive. To really fete a bestie, you need to give a proper toast.

Guests gushing (and soon swaying). Bestie blushing. Friendship locked.

In case you're not a toasting natural, here's a lazy formula:

1. "You all know that we're here to celebrate [bestie's] [occasion/accomplishment]. But the celebration would be half-baked if we didn't take a moment to discuss the matter and raise our glasses a few times."

2. "Now, there are countless ways to describe how special [bestie] is to all of us. [Insert three generic modifiers like 'witty, dashing, and spunky'] come to mind."

3. "But I'm no wordsmith, so I thought we'd go around the table to each contribute a few adjectives to the toast. So, tell us, what are the first three words that pop into *your* mind when you think of [bestie]?"

4. "Oh, and let's raise our glasses to toast [bestie] after each person's contribution! Cheryl, why don't you start?. . . ."

Even carbophobes will be tempted by this harissa-accented potato salad. Smashing the potatoes with the back of a bowl will not only give them a casual look but also provides extra surface area to absorb the vibrant dressing.

SERVES 4
SKILL LEVEL 2

2 pounds baby Yukon Gold potatoes

Kosher salt

¼ cup mayonnaise

¼ cup crème fraîche

¼ cup harissa

2 tablespoons finely chopped preserved lemon

1 cup fresh flat-leaf parsley, coarsely chopped

HARISSA POTATO SALAD

1
Place the potatoes in a large pot and cover with water by 1 inch. Add a handful of salt and bring to a boil. Reduce the heat to maintain a simmer and cook until tender, 20 to 25 minutes. Drain and let cool slightly.

2
Transfer the potatoes to a rimmed sheet pan and lightly smash each one with the bottom of a small bowl to flatten slightly, until bite-size.

3
Meanwhile, in a large bowl, whisk together the mayonnaise, crème fraîche, harissa, and preserved lemon. Add the warm potatoes and parsley. Season with salt and toss. Serve warm or at room temperature.

The texture of this "flatbread" is floppier than the original but it's an unexpected creation that's fun to eat and flexible for topping with just about anything on hand. The recipe below demonstrates a few simple pantry ingredients that make sense for this menu. Experiment freely! Think smoked salmon and capers; pomegranate, feta, and chopped pistachios; or sesame seeds and jalapeños. We like to have more than one sheet pan on hand so everyone can freestyle and make their own.

SERVES 4
SKILL LEVEL 3

INSTANT SPICED-YOGURT "FLATBREAD"

1 (6-ounce) container full-fat Greek yogurt

1 tablespoon all-purpose flour

½ teaspoon, plus 1 tablespoon olive oil, plus more for the pan

½ teaspoon paprika

½ teaspoon cumin seeds or fennel seeds

¼ teaspoon red pepper flakes

1

Preheat the oven to 400°F. Line a sheet pan with parchment paper and lightly oil it.

2

Open the yogurt and add the flour and ½ teaspoon of the olive oil to the container and stir to make a thick batter. Using a rubber spatula, evenly spread the batter out on the prepared sheet pan into a thin 10-inch circle or square. Drizzle the batter with the remaining 1 tablespoon olive oil and sprinkle with the paprika, cumin seeds or fennel seeds, and red pepper flakes. Bake until lightly browned and set, about 15 minutes.

3

Let cool for 5 minutes; cut or tear the flatbread into pieces to serve.

1 ripe golden pineapple

3 tablespoons sugar

1 tablespoon ground cinnamon

4 tablespoons (½ stick) unsalted butter

The menu goes out the way it came in: with lush flavors that lean on strong spices for depth and heft. This dessert is deceptively simple, but watch the pineapple carefully while broiling, since the cinnamon-sugar turns from light brown to burnt rather quickly.

BUTTERY CARAMELIZED PINEAPPLE WITH CINNAMON

1
Preheat the broiler and place the oven rack 6 inches from the heating element. Line a sheet pan with parchment paper.

2
Quarter the pineapple lengthwise, keeping the top attached to each piece. Lay each quarter cut-side down and cut into the wedge at an angle to remove the core from the center; discard the core. Carefully cut the fruit away from the skin in one piece. Wrap the green tops in aluminum foil. Lay each quarter skin-side down on the prepared sheet pan, then place the fruit back on top of its skin. Cut the fruit crosswise into ¾-inch slices.

3
Mix together the sugar and cinnamon in a small bowl. Sprinkle the top of each pineapple quarter with approximately 1 tablespoon of the cinnamon-sugar.

4
Broil the pineapple quarters until lightly browned, 5 to 7 minutes. Remove the foil to expose the leaves on the pineapple tops. Immediately place 1 tablespoon of the butter on each quarter to melt, then serve.

A Modern Retro Dinner

MENU

In old Hollywood, agents used to say that no one ever got anywhere without a schtick. Sure, you can become a legendary entertainer among your friends by hosting only chic, understated affairs. But it's also fun to slip into a schtick of your own by hosting a dinner with a vintage theme. Now, don't confuse this with a "theme party," that costume-rental affair with craft-store decorations and games to match. We mean a retrograde evening of once-fashionable dishes brought forward in time with a tweak or a twist (of grapefruit, for instance, like in the Harvey Wallbanger variation you'll pour).

The menu throws back to a supposedly simpler party past, when cocktails were stiff, meat was red, and dressing was green (Green *Goddess*—for the crudités). We're sure that hazy era felt just as complicated as life does today, but you won't be stopped from devouring the "outdated" vibes of a rib eye in Caesar butter served with spinach salad warmed by pancetta dressing alongside a Gruyère Dutch baby.

When folks start to question your combination of culinary eras, explain that this throwback dinner is date nonspecific, because historical accuracy is not your end. No, no: A German chocolate icebox cake is, like history, welcome to repeat itself for a second helping.

Skill Level

The rib eye is for your most nimble of guests: It will take someone with their wits about them to execute not only the steak but also the Caesar butter and Dutch baby.

Special Equipment

- Punch bowl

- Silicone ice cube trays

- 12-inch and 10-inch cast-iron skillets

- Stand mixer

- Bamboo cocktail skewers

- 18 x 13–inch rimmed sheet pan

The menu throws back to a supposedly simpler party past, when cocktails were stiff, meat was red, and dressing was green.

Explain that this throwback dinner is date nonspecific, because historical accuracy is not your end.

Game Plan

- **The Night Before:** Make the Campari ice cubes and cake

- **Three Hours Before:** Prepare the Caesar butter

- **One Hour Before:** Prepare the rib eye

- **45 Minutes Before:** Make the crudités

- **30 Minutes Before:** Make the spinach salad and shallots

- **As the Guests Arrive:** Make the Wallbangers

- **Right After the Steak Is Done:** Make the Dutch baby

Wine Ideas

What's more old-school than a Mosel Kabinett Riesling and a red Bordeaux? Historically, these are a few of the most classic wines of Europe. The lightly fruity and very crisp Riesling for the greens on the table and the cheesy Dutch baby. And a classic hearty and dry Bordeaux for the rib eye is an easy match.

The Campari ice cubes in this recipe may seem fussy, but they're a winner in the visuals department (especially highlighted in your mother's hand-me-down punch bowl), so be sure to get them going the night before your party. For easiest unmolding, use silicone ice cube trays (which you should have anyway, as they'll advance your cocktail game permanently). Extra credit: Use two different cube sizes (we recommend two trays with 2-inch cubes and two trays with 1-inch cubes).

MAKES 12 to 14 cocktails

SKILL LEVEL 2

2 cups Campari

2¼ cups fresh grapefruit juice

1¼ cups vodka

⅓ cup Galliano

GRAPEFRUIT HARVEY WALLBANGERS

1
Pour the Campari and 6 cups water into a pitcher and stir to combine. Pour the mixture into ice cube trays (see headnote) and freeze until set, at least 6 hours, though overnight is best.

2
Combine the grapefruit juice, vodka, and Galliano in a punch bowl. Just before guests arrive, add the large Campari ice cubes to the punch. Leave the smaller cubes in the freezer for serving in each glass.

Crudités can be wonderfully refreshing, but a platter of crispy veg will warrant only a cocktail-hour shrug unless it's accompanied by a creamy green bowl of punchy herb dressing. The anchovies are optional if you're planning to play kissing games after dinner, but they're also called for in the Caesar butter on the steaks so you might as well lean in. To really wow, choose unexpected vegetables, like fennel, spears of jicama, loose leaves of endive, or even fingers of kohlrabi (gasp).

CRUDITÉS WITH MODERN GREEN GODDESS

SERVES 6
SKILL LEVEL 2

1

Combine the cilantro, parsley, 2½ tablespoons of the chives, the tarragon, anchovies (if desired), serrano pepper, and garlic in a food processor and pulse several times to finely chop and combine. Add the lemon zest and juice, yogurt, and olive oil and pulse until smooth. Season to taste with salt and black pepper.

2

Serve topped with the remaining ½ tablespoon chopped chives, accompanied by the vegetables.

¼ cup packed fresh cilantro leaves

¼ cup packed fresh parsley leaves

3 tablespoons coarsely chopped fresh chives

2 tablespoons chopped fresh tarragon

2 anchovy fillets, drained (optional)

1 serrano pepper, stemmed and seeded

½ garlic clove, smashed

Zest and juice of 1 lemon

1 cup full-fat Greek yogurt

3 tablespoons olive oil

Kosher salt and freshly ground black pepper

3 cups mixed raw vegetables (like radishes, cauliflower, romanesco, endive, green beans, small carrots, turnips, and/or broccoli, cut into pieces as necessary)

SERVES 6
SKILL LEVEL 3

There's something satisfying and vaguely alchemical about the way a hot oil dressing lightly wilts the feisty spinach leaves in this salad. The moment it's dressed, the dish transforms to a slightly shiny, beautiful salad unlike the bowl of dull leaves that were just mocking you with their bounce and volume. You can prepare the salad ahead of time for ease, but don't dress it until the moment you're about to serve.

SPINACH SALAD WITH HOT PANCETTA DRESSING

1 pound spinach, washed and trimmed

2 apples, cored and diced

10 ounces cremini mushrooms, thinly sliced

¾ cup crumbled Gorgonzola cheese

½ cup chopped toasted walnuts

¼ cup plus 2 tablespoons chopped fresh chives

2 tablespoons olive oil

8 ounces pancetta, thinly sliced and chopped

3 shallots, finely chopped

⅔ cup apple cider vinegar

2 tablespoons whole-grain mustard

1 tablespoon sugar

Kosher salt and freshly ground black pepper

1

Toss the spinach with the apples, mushrooms, ½ cup of the Gorgonzola, ¼ cup of the walnuts, and ¼ cup of the chives in a serving bowl and set aside.

2

Heat the olive oil over medium-high heat in a small pot. Add the pancetta and cook, stirring often, until crisp, 8 to 10 minutes. Using a slotted spoon, transfer the pancetta to a paper towel–lined plate.

3

Add the shallots to the pot with the pancetta fat and cook until just softened, 1 to 2 minutes. Whisk in the vinegar, mustard, sugar, and salt and pepper. Continue whisking until heated, about 30 seconds. Pour over the spinach immediately and toss. Sprinkle the remaining ¼ cup Gorgonzola, ¼ cup walnuts, 2 tablespoons chives, and the crumbled pancetta over the top and serve.

Trust us: You're going to love the Caesar butter, so make extra. It freezes beautifully as a plastic-wrapped log and can be added to steamed veggies or spread on bread and toasted in the oven for a quick cocktail bite when a friend stops by unexpectedly one afternoon. Note: To properly cook a 2-inch-thick steak, it's critical that the steaks be completely at room temperature before they're cooked. And don't slice into them after cooking until they've rested for 20 minutes.

RIB EYE WITH CAESAR BUTTER

SERVES 6
SKILL LEVEL 5

FOR THE CAESAR BUTTER

2 garlic cloves

2 anchovy fillets (deboned if necessary)

Zest and juice of 1 lemon

1 tablespoon Dijon mustard

2 teaspoons Worcestershire sauce

Freshly ground black pepper

¼ cup grated Parmesan cheese

½ cup (1 stick) unsalted butter, cut into several pieces, at room temperature

Kosher salt

FOR THE RIB EYES

2 (2-inch-thick) bone-in rib eye steaks (about 4 pounds total), at room temperature

Kosher salt and freshly ground black pepper

6 tablespoons olive oil

6 garlic cloves

2 sprigs thyme

1 lemon

1

MAKE THE CAESAR BUTTER: In a food processor, combine the garlic, anchovies, lemon zest and juice, Dijon mustard, Worcestershire, and 1½ teaspoons pepper and pulse until a thick, homogeneous paste forms. Add the Parmesan and butter and pulse until fully incorporated and smooth. Season with salt and transfer to a small bowl or ramekin. Refrigerate until dinnertime.

2

MAKE THE RIB EYES: Before your guests arrive, take the rib eyes and the Caesar butter out of the fridge to allow them to come to room temperature. One hour before dinner, season each rib eye with 1 tablespoon salt and 1 teaspoon pepper.

3

Preheat the oven to 400°F. Line a rimmed sheet pan with a wire rack.

4

Heat a 12-inch cast-iron or heavy-bottomed skillet over medium-high heat for 10 minutes. Add 3 tablespoons olive oil to the skillet. When the oil just begins to smoke, place one steak in the skillet, standing it up on its "fat cap" side, and sear until the fat starts to render and turns golden brown, about 4 minutes. Lay the steak on one side in the skillet and sear for another

RECIPE CONTINUES

5 minutes. Flip and sear for an additional 5 minutes. Add 2 tablespoons of the Caesar butter, 3 cloves of garlic, and 1 sprig of thyme and baste the steak constantly with the melted butter for another 2 minutes.

5

Transfer the steak to the prepared sheet pan. Tip out the fat remaining in the pan, wipe the pan clean, and proceed to cook the second steak in the exact same way.

Transfer the sheet pan with the steaks to the oven and cook for 10 minutes, or until an instant-read thermometer registers 120°F.

6

Squeeze the lemon over the steaks, then allow them to rest for 20 minutes. Cut the meat off the bone in one piece, then slice it against the grain, about a ½-inch thick; serve family-style on a platter dolloped with the Caesar butter.

6 Questions
to Get the Table Talking

Host a dinner party, and your guests will leave with a hazy memory of a nice evening. Host a *conversation* at your dinner party, and guests will remember new people, heated exchanges, and hearty laughs.

Here are a few standbys:

1. "What title will you give your eventual memoirs? Mine would be called *Always the Host, Never the Guest*."

2. "If you were a drag queen, what would your stage name be? I've always admired Visa Declined."

3. For conservative affairs, try, "What advice would you give your ten-year-old self?" or "What ridiculous invention do you wish you had thought of?"

4. For a think-tanker, ask, "What is the last mind-blowing statistic you read?" or "What's the best podcast no one at this table has heard of?"

5. With a confident crowd, ask, "What humiliating thing did you do in the distant past that still makes you cringe when you think of it today?"

6. For a spicy crowd, ask, "Who's your celebrity 'hall pass'?" If you don't know what that means, don't ask this question.

A Dutch baby is a showstopping, puffy cousin of the popover or Yorkshire pudding. But that puff only lasts a few minutes, so coordinate its baking to coincide with the moment everyone sits to eat for a dramatic arrival at the table. Preheat the skillet in the oven while the steaks cook, then crank the heat to 450°F as soon as the steaks come out, *carefully* fill the now-hot skillet with the batter, and get ready for the puff.

GRUYÈRE DUTCH BABY

SERVES 6
SKILL LEVEL 4

3 large eggs, at room temperature

¾ cup whole milk, at room temperature

⅔ cup all-purpose flour

Kosher salt and freshly ground black pepper

3 scallions, sliced

2 tablespoons unsalted butter

2 ounces Gruyère cheese, finely grated (about ¼ cup)

1

Preheat the oven to 450°F and place a 10-inch cast-iron skillet in the oven to preheat for 25 minutes.

2

In a blender, combine the eggs, milk, flour, 1 teaspoon salt, and 1 teaspoon pepper and blend on high for 1 minute. Add two-thirds of the sliced scallions and pulse a few more times until incorporated.

3

Remove the skillet from the oven and add the butter, swirling to coat the sides of the skillet. Immediately pour the batter into the hot skillet, top with the grated cheese, return the skillet to the oven, and bake until puffed and golden brown, about 20 minutes.

4

Cut into wedges and serve hot in the skillet, topped with the remaining scallions.

The bacon in this recipe does double duty, since its rendered fat cooks the shallots and the crispy bits garnish the finished dish. If your bacon didn't give off a lot of fat, just add a couple tablespoons of olive oil. And buy fattier bacon next time.

SERVES 6
SKILL LEVEL 3

GLAZED SHALLOTS WITH BACON AND THYME

2 strips thick-cut bacon (about 4 ounces), cut into ½-inch pieces

Olive oil (optional)

18 medium shallots (about 1¼ pounds)

Kosher salt

1½ cups chicken stock

½ cup sherry vinegar

2 tablespoons sugar

2 teaspoons fresh thyme leaves

1

In a large heavy-bottomed skillet, fry the bacon over medium-high heat until crisp, about 5 minutes. Using a slotted spoon, transfer the bacon to a paper towel–lined plate, leaving the fat behind.

2

If the pan seems dry, add a few tablespoons of olive oil to the bacon fat to coat the bottom of the pan. Add the shallots and 1 teaspoon salt to the skillet and sear, turning occasionally, until golden brown in spots, 6 to 8 minutes.

3

Add the chicken stock, sherry vinegar, sugar, and half the thyme leaves and bring to a boil. Reduce the heat to maintain a simmer, cover partially with a lid, and cook for 10 minutes. Remove the lid and simmer, turning the shallots occasionally, until the sauce has reduced and the shallots are soft and glazed, 10 to 15 minutes more.

4

Taste and adjust the seasoning. Serve garnished with the bacon and remaining thyme leaves.

2½ cups cold heavy cream

⅓ cup sugar

2 teaspoons coconut extract

Kosher salt

1⅔ cups coconut flakes

⅔ cup pecans

1 package chocolate wafers, such as Nabisco Famous Wafers (about 40 cookies)

Maldon salt

This cake is actually an easy assembly project of cookies and whipped cream, so give it to your least foodie friend to tackle if you're crowdsourcing dishes for this menu. (They'll appreciate the confidence boost.) But it should set for at least 5 hours (or, better, overnight) to achieve a cakey texture, so warn your friend not to procrastinate on their assignment.

GERMAN CHOCOLATE ICEBOX CAKE

1

Preheat the oven to 350°F.

2

In the chilled bowl of a stand mixer fitted with the whisk attachment, combine the heavy cream, sugar, coconut extract, and a pinch of kosher salt. Beat until medium peaks form. Fold 1 cup of the coconut flakes into the cream and set aside.

3

Meanwhile, toast the remaining coconut and the pecans on a rimmed sheet pan for 8 minutes. Coarsely chop the pecans and let cool. Set aside.

4

Working on a large serving platter, spread a chocolate wafer with about 2 teaspoons of the coconut cream, then repeat, and stack the wafers together, building a log 20 cookies in length. Repeat to form a second log directly below and parallel to the first, forming a rectangle.

5

Cover the entire cake with the remaining coconut cream, being sure to cover all visible cookies. Using a damp paper towel, clean up the edges of the platter and refrigerate the cake, uncovered, for at least 5 hours or up to overnight.

6

Just before serving, sprinkle the toasted coconut and pecans on the top and sides of the cake. Sprinkle a pinch of Maldon salt over the top of the cake. Slice the cake on an angle, revealing the interior stripes.

A Friday Night Feast

MENU

There's something electric about a Friday night dinner party, with its promise of an extra night of fun and fury. After a long week of work, the first drink lands a little softer; the appetizer tastes more tantalizing; the faces of gathered friends glow a bit brighter. The weekend will come alive as collars are loosened and conference call trauma fades as someone commandeers the Sonos system and the meal makes its way to the table.

This menu goes out to all those kids who just moved to the city and got that new apartment. To everyone whose dinner party ambitions exceed their glassware count (you'll simply serve beer can cocktails!). To anyone who's angry at all their friends and wants to make some new ones (for tonight, for Instagram, really).

Friday night's promise of an A+ party will look effortless, because this isn't your first time to the slow cooker rodeo (or maybe it is! Who cares, you're young!). You'll serve a slightly sweet adobo that readied itself while you took the bedroom door off its hinges to form a tabletop on sawhorses. You'll play with Mexican- and Asian-inspired flavors across the menu, because experimentation is your thing. You'll sear avocados on a hot skillet and toss Chex Mix in duck fat, because who knew that was a thing? (You did, of course.)

People will be late (they worked all day, after all) and the neighbors will complain about the music (it's hard not to be jealous), but you've got chocolate chip cookies with a salted caramel mezcal crema for dessert. And Monday seems a century away.

Skill Level

Those with the least experience should work on the radishes and rice. The avocados and bok choy need a little more experience. Someone should be appointed to make sure the guests don't eat all the cookies before dinner.

Special Equipment

- Slow cooker or Instant Pot

- 12-inch cast-iron skillet

- Stand mixer

- Two 18 x 13–inch rimmed sheet pans

Game Plan

- **The Night Before:** Make the cookies

- **Three Hours Before:** Prepare the adobo

- **One Hour Before:** Prepare the Chex Mix

- **45 Minutes Before:** Make the radishes

- **30 Minutes Before:** Make the rice

- **20 Minutes Before:** Make the bok choy

- **10 Minutes Before:** Make the avocados

- **As the Guests Arrive:** Make the shandy

After a long week of work, the first drink lands a little softer; the appetizer tastes more tantalizing; the faces of gathered friends glow a bit brighter.

Wine Ideas

Riesling is perfect for this menu, but choose a dry and mineral Austrian Riesling to match the rich, spicy flavors on the table. For a more interesting pairing, pick up an Italian Nebbiolo from the Piedmont region to offer a spicy kick with the Filipino adobo.

Pro-Tip: Eco Chic

- **Plates:** If you're feeling lazy or casual or simply don't want to borrow extra plates from a neighbor, use disposable bamboo plates, which are available online and aren't too expensive. They're biodegradable and look great (rustic, almost) compared to soggy paper or eco-ugly plastic.

- **Napkins:** Most people avoid the fuss of cloth dinner napkins. The only thing that makes them fussy, though, is the idea that they'll stain easily and require ironing. Forget the starched white linen napkins and buy a set of non-white or patterned cotton napkins that are meant to look rustic and un-ironed. Even a collection of waffle-fabric kitchen towels look chic folded at a place setting.

This spicy cocktail is a fusion of a michelada and shandy. Best of all, the drink is mixed and enjoyed right from the can or bottle, so there are no glasses required. These cocktails work best if they're made as you go, so having a DIY station set up will be key. Just be careful when inverting the cans or bottles.

MAKES 16 cocktails
SKILL LEVEL 1

Kosher salt

Zest of 1 lime

16 cans or bottles Mexican beer, like Modelo Especial or Corona

Cholula hot sauce

4 bottles Jarritos grapefruit soda, or other grapefruit soda

MEXICAN SHANDY

1

On a small plate, mix together salt and the lime zest and set aside.

2

For each cocktail, open the beer and empty it down just past the neck, either by pouring a bit into a pitcher to be served later or just by taking a few sips (if it's your own drink). Add 3 pinches of lime zest salt and 3 dashes of hot sauce. Fill the beer back up to the opening with grapefruit soda. Place your thumb over the top and (carefully!) invert the beer to mix the ingredients. Serve directly in the can or bottle.

We've been riffing on this snack mix at Tasting Table since we first published the original recipe from Jake Godby, of Humphry Slocombe ice cream, at Truck Stop in San Francisco nearly a decade ago. Find duck fat at your local butcher or order it easily online—and order extra, since you'll make this more than once!

SERVES 8
SKILL LEVEL 2

DUCK FAT CHEX MIX

½ cup rendered duck fat, melted

1 teaspoon Worcestershire sauce

1½ teaspoons smoked salt

½ teaspoon garlic powder

½ teaspoon onion powder

½ teaspoon freshly ground black pepper

Pinch of cayenne pepper

3 cups Corn Chex

3 cups Rice Chex

1½ cups Wheat Chex

1 cup small pretzels

3 sprigs thyme

1

Preheat the oven to 250°F.

2

In a medium bowl, stir together the melted duck fat, Worcestershire, smoked salt, garlic powder, onion powder, black pepper, and cayenne to combine.

3

On a large roasting pan or rimmed sheet pan, combine the Corn Chex, Rice Chex, Wheat Chex, pretzels, and thyme sprigs. Drizzle the duck fat–spice mixture over the top and use a rubber spatula to toss and coat the Chex evenly. Bake, stirring every 15 minutes, until the Chex mix is toasted and fragrant, about 1 hour. Remove the pan from the oven and serve warm. (Cooled Chex mix can be rewarmed in a 250°F oven until warmed through, about 7 minutes.)

2 oranges

6 pounds pork shoulder, cut
into 2-inch pieces

2 cups soy sauce

1½ cups rice vinegar

½ cup toasted sesame oil

½ cup packed light
brown sugar

12 whole cloves

8 garlic cloves, smashed

6 bay leaves

4 star anise pods

4 tablespoons peanut oil,
divided

Pork shoulder is one of the most cost-effective large-format meats you can buy for a party. Remember that cheap meat requires slow cooking to turn tough into tender while producing a soppy sauce that turns your guests into a hype committee for your cooking skills. This Filipino spin on a dish many Americans usually think of as Mexican is a perfect demonstration.

SLOW-COOKED FILIPINO ADOBO

1

Remove just the outermost peel of the oranges using a vegetable peeler.

2

In a large bowl, toss the pork with the soy sauce, 2 cups water, the rice vinegar, sesame oil, brown sugar, cloves, garlic, bay leaves, star anise, and orange peels. Marinate for 1 hour.

3

Line a plate with paper towels. Using a slotted spoon, transfer the pork to the prepared plate and pat dry. Reserve the marinating liquid.

4

In a 6-quart Dutch oven or slow cooker, heat 2 tablespoons of the peanut oil over medium-high heat. Add half the pork and cook, turning frequently, until browned on all sides, 6 to 8 minutes. Place the browned pork on a plate and repeat the browning process with the remaining 2 tablespoons peanut oil and pork.

5

Add all of the browned pork and the reserved marinating liquid to a slow cooker or return them to the Dutch oven. Bring to a simmer and cook, covered, until tender when pierced with a fork, 1 to 1½ hours.

3 cups jasmine rice

1½ teaspoons kosher salt

Sure, it's "just rice," but you'll need it to sop up all that delicious sauce from the adobo.

JASMINE RICE

1

Rinse the rice in a fine-mesh sieve until the water runs clear. Drain.

2

Combine the rice, 6 cups water, and the salt in a medium pot. Bring to a boil, reduce the heat to maintain a simmer, and cover with a lid. Cook for 20 minutes, until the water has been absorbed. Fluff with a fork before serving.

1 bunch radishes

1 tablespoon rice vinegar

2 tablespoons soy sauce

2 teaspoons toasted sesame seeds

2 teaspoons sugar

1 teaspoon toasted sesame oil

Any braise worth its sauce will benefit from a bit of texture and crunch. Hence, these quick pickles.

QUICK-PICKLED SESAME-AND-SOY RADISHES

Slice the radishes into very thin rounds and place in a glass bowl. Add the remaining ingredients and toss to combine. Let sit for 15 minutes before serving.

These seared avocados are another head-turner, with their dramatic dark faces and pale, creamy centers. Keep careful watch during cooking: The chili powder will darken quickly once it hits the pan and you don't want it to completely blacken, or it will become bitter tasting.

SEARED AVOCADOS

5 avocados

1 tablespoon chili powder

½ cup sour cream

1 tablespoon fresh lime juice

Kosher salt

Cilantro sprigs, for garnish

1

Cut the avocados in half and remove the pits. Sprinkle the cut side of each half with chili powder. Place the avocados, cut-side down, on a cast-iron skillet over medium-high heat; cook until well browned, about 2 minutes.

2

In a small bowl, mix the sour cream, lime juice, and 1 tablespoon water.

3

Place the avocados on a plate, sprinkle with salt, drizzle with the crema, and garnish with cilantro sprigs.

¼ cup peanut oil

6 garlic cloves, thinly sliced

2 tablespoons minced fresh ginger

6 scallions, coarsely chopped

1 teaspoon red pepper flakes

2 cups chopped pineapple

Kosher salt

2 pounds baby bok choy, halved with root end kept intact

1 to 2 tablespoons fish sauce

If you can't find a fresh pineapple out of season, drained canned pineapple chunks or rings will work in this dish, since the bok choy is the title character in the show.

BOK CHOY WITH PINEAPPLE AND CRISPY GARLIC

1

In a large skillet, stir together the cold oil and garlic. Place over medium heat and cook, stirring occasionally, until the garlic is crispy, about 6 minutes. Using a slotted spoon, transfer the garlic to a paper towel–lined plate.

2

Return the skillet with the oil to medium-high heat. Add the ginger, scallions, and red pepper flakes and cook, stirring, until lightly browned, about 4 minutes. Add the pineapple and cook, stirring occasionally, until lightly browned, about 6 minutes.

3

Meanwhile, bring a large pot of salted water to a boil. Add the bok choy and cook, stirring occasionally, until bright green and just tender, about 2 minutes. Drain.

4

Add the drained bok choy and fish sauce to the skillet and cook, stirring, until combined. Transfer to a platter and garnish with the crispy garlic. Serve hot or at room temperature.

This dough is easiest to work with if it has rested in the fridge for at least 2 hours. Thankfully, the recipe makes a lot of cookies and cream, though you'll be surprised how many disappear as your guests realize how tasty they are.

SERVES 8
SKILL LEVEL 3

CHOCOLATE CHIP COOKIES WITH SALTED CARAMEL MEZCAL CREMA

FOR THE COOKIES

2½ cups all-purpose flour, plus more for dusting

¾ teaspoon baking soda

¼ teaspoon kosher salt

1 cup (2 sticks) unsalted butter, at room temperature

1 cup packed light brown sugar

¾ cup granulated sugar

1 teaspoon vanilla extract

2 large eggs, at room temperature

14 ounces semisweet chocolate, coarsely chopped into ½- to 1-inch chunks

FOR THE CREMA

1½ cups salted caramel sauce (such as Stonewall Kitchen)

2 cups crème fraîche or sour cream

1 tablespoon mezcal

1

MAKE THE COOKES: In a medium bowl, whisk together the flour, baking soda, and salt. Set aside.

2

In the bowl of a stand mixer fitted with the paddle attachment, beat the butter with the brown sugar, granulated sugar, and vanilla on medium speed just until smooth. Beat in the eggs until thoroughly incorporated, then blend in the flour mixture and the chocolate chunks.

3

On a lightly floured work surface, divide the dough into quarters. Shape each piece into a log about 9 inches long. Wrap the logs in plastic wrap and refrigerate until firm, at least 2 hours and preferably 24 hours. (The dough logs can be refrigerated for up to 1 week or frozen for up to 1 month.)

4

Position racks in the upper and lower thirds of the oven and preheat the oven to 350°F. Line two sheet pans with parchment paper or silicone baking mats.

5

Slice 2 dough logs into ¾-inch-thick disks and place the disks 3 inches apart on the prepared sheet pans. If the chips fall out, simply push them back in. Bake the cookies, rotating

RECIPE CONTINUES

the pans midway through baking, until very lightly browned in the centers, 10 to 15 minutes.

6

Let the cookies cool on the pans until firm enough to handle, then use a spatula to transfer them to a wire rack. Repeat with the remaining 2 logs of dough. The baked cookies will keep well in an airtight container at room temperature for up to 4 days.

7

MAKE THE CREMA: Combine the caramel, crème fraîche, and mezcal in a small bowl, and stir well. Spoon a little onto one side of each cookie or serve on the side as a dipping sauce.

Coda

Lipstick-stained glasses. An only-the-bone-left T-bone. Wadded-up napkins and spent corks. The stuff of dinner party aftermath.

But it's in the wake of the chatter and the fever-pitched din that it comes—the second wind. The magic is far from over.

We naturally end up back in the kitchen. Elbows on the counter. There's only of few of us left, the party's core. A subtle quiet descends as the chitchat gets a bit more serious, more candid. We review the night's menu and recap the foibles. The chicken probably cooked 10 minutes too long. Wish we had doubled the kale salad. Oh shit, we should've invited so-and-so! There's always next time. And the time after that.

But somehow, we're still hungry tonight.

For something more. Something simple, nourishing—to amp up our restored energy. An unplanned ransack of the fridge and cupboards ensues. In the darkness, the gleam of the open fridge is somehow a beckoning comfort. We find a little of this, a little of that. The leftover detritus of other dinners, other brunches. There's ALWAYS pasta and a can of tomatoes around. But we want to augment those flavors, make them late-night fodder. Not just stick-to-your-ribs: stick-to-your-soul.

A little more rooting around turns up salty, canned good things: plump capers, tinned anchovies, a dry salami.

The ultimate lusty-late-night dish dawns upon us: pasta puttanesca.

Perfect. No recipe needed.

The kitchen simmers with activity.

For people who never have time for anything, tonight we seem to have all the time in world. Everything goes into one big pot. We don't even boil the penne separately—just cook it right in the sloppy sauce. The starch exudes and melds everything together. Kind of like us, chilly beer in hand, while we all eat out of the pot. Together.

—Todd Coleman, 2019

ONE-POT PUTTANESCA

½ cup good-quality extra-virgin olive oil

½ cup pitted black olives, coarsely chopped

6 garlic cloves, thinly sliced

1 box penne pasta

1 (28-ounce) can whole peeled tomatoes, crushed lightly with your (clean) hand or a spoon

½ cup sliced salami

6 tablespoons capers (rinsed if they're salted, drained if they're brined)

1 teaspoon kosher salt

1 teaspoon red pepper flakes

Good handful of fresh basil, torn into smaller pieces

Parmesan cheese

1
Combine the olive oil, olives, and garlic in a large, wide saucepan or Dutch oven. Turn the heat to high and cook, stirring, until the garlic starts to take on a little color and the olives are a little crispy, about 3 minutes.

2
Add everything else except the cheese (yes, including the pasta!) plus 3 cups water, bring to a boil, and then cook, stirring occasionally, until the pasta is al dente, and serve with Parmesan.

Morning-After
Checklist

- Sleep late; order breakfast in; bask in the majesty of your successful party.

- Pull out all the personal effects you hid last-minute under beds, in closets, on top of the fridge.

- Think of any connections you promised to make among guests and note them before your sieve-like mind drains (but don't send those connection emails until Monday morning, when everyone's fresh).

- Drop a concise text message to anyone who brought a host gift or bottle of wine to acknowledge their thoughtfulness (end your text with "xoxo" as in a note card so they know they're not expected to respond while they have a headache).

- Draft a follow-up note to all the guests thanking them for the terrific party and providing links to any books, music, apps, or podcasts that were discussed as a group (and any good group photos taken!) and suggesting that you all "do it again soon"; maybe someone will take the hint and invite you back.

Responsible Rides

We aren't apologetic that we believe strong cocktails and free-flowing wine and beer are a critical component of most party magic, so many heavy-drinking jokes are tucked into the pages of this book. But don't forget that *not every guest drinks* and, for those who do, *you are responsible for their ability to leave your party safely*, both ethically and, probably, legally:

- Most parties will have at least one person who doesn't drink or is taking a month off for health reasons. **Always have a few booze-free beverages prominently available** at the bar, like ginger beer, flavored Perrier, and sodas.

- Always **offer arriving guests "a drink," not a "cocktail,"** as in, "Can I offer you a drink? We've got a gin cocktail, a cabernet sauvignon, and some nice sodas and juices at the bar." That gives non-drinkers the chance to accept your offer without needing to explain that they don't drink alcohol. If you notice non-drinkers during cocktail hour, add a couple of carafes of sparkling mineral water to the dinner table, too.

- **You must ensure everyone driving home is sober before they leave,** and shoving a coffee into a drunk guy's hand doesn't count. In the age of Uber and Lyft, it's easier than ever to quietly order a car, plug in your guest's home address, and shove the boozy rake into the safe ride. You'll be thanked in the morning.

- **Pro-tip:** As the party progresses and you notice that some guests who drove are getting tipsy, offer them their next cocktail only on the condition that they first surrender their car keys.

Acknowledgments

We owe enormous gratitude to our colleagues and friends who helped make this book possible:

Our talented and creative recipe developers helped form and shape these menus, including our star food stylist and good friend Andrea Slonecker, Molly Baz, Katie Foster, Devon Gaffney, Lauren Palmeri, Nora Singley, and Lauren Utvich. Special thanks to Alex Alan for his expert wine pairings throughout.

Our indefatigable recipe testers triple-checked and photographed over a hundred recipes in one kitchen in four days. Thank you, Kristina Preka, Alison Cancro, Megan Cornell, and Dave Katz (photography).

Dozens of people tested these menus, including many Tasting Table teammates who spent their weekends cooking with *their* friends, including Andrew Bui, Adrienne Castro, Bertha Chen, Nisha Chittal, Erin Keene, Angela Lee, Margaret Lunetta, Abby Reisner, Nikhil Shah, Colbern Uhl, Vashti Viray, and Nime Walbe La-Fauci.

The beautiful photography throughout the book is thanks to our hyper-organized team of stylists, photo gurus, cooks, and assistants, including Andrea Slonecker (food stylist), Ashley Toth (prop stylist), Vanessa Rojo de la Vega (photo), Michelle Xue Sun (photo), Vance Spicer (video), Mira Evnine (food stylist), Megan Cornell (food assistant), Karintha Jimenez-Grune (food assistant), Jackie Tris (food assistant), Jordan Runcie-Hubbard (production assistant), Jasper Rosenheim (production assistant), Luz Dary Gil Salgado (facilities), and Patricia Cesar-Sandoval (facilities).

The parties came to life when our gorgeous friends joined us for a few days of dinner party shooting, including Grace Atwood, Caleb Thill, Jackie Gebel, Juliana Kleist-Mendez, Jacob Miller, Dan Fratoni, Haisu Qu, Mathé Kamsutchorn, Artyom Koldeznoy,

Quentin Perry, Dan Churchill, Elyse Kellogg, Gregory Kellogg, Vashti Viray, Matthew Rice, Delia Mooney, Aaron Hutcherson, Kristyn Moss, Danielle Rind, Annie Salsich, Colbern Uhl, Tashi Chontso, Tsering Dorjay, Chelsea Grace Miller, Jacqueline Warshawer, Andrew Warshawer, Tadashi Ono, Dominic Bracco, Summer Bracco, Anna Polonsky, Fernando Aciar, Adrienne Castro, Brooke Altman, Betsy Chen, Marcus Washington, Patrick Guetle, Amelia Skarloff, Ryan Balas, Deirdre Balas, Bertha Chen, Ana Lucia Cano, Miguel Lara, Gaeleen Quinn, and Pablo Goldberg.

Thank you to Gary's Loft for providing the backdrop to all the lifestyle photography. And to Ralph Lauren for the use of their beautiful home products, furniture, and bar cart. A special shout-out to Breads Bakery, EMILY Restaurant, and Meatball Shop for keeping our photoshoot team well fed. And very special thanks to Hallie Manheim for sourcing our food partners and involving so many Instagram influencers in the shoot.

Gratitude and admiration to everyone who contributed ideas, provided feedback, edited drafts, and indulged Geoff politely when he wouldn't stop texting variations of his rambling text throughout 2017: Kai Mathey, Abby Reisner, Jane Frye, Brooke Welsch, Steven Cutler, Javier Martinez, Claire Hoffman, Sam Masters, Will Brewer, Markus Kirschner, Sara Molnar, and Lenny Addamo.

And finally, thank you to our book team, who forced this book into existence: Kara Rota, Will Schwalbe, Bryn Clark, and Andrea Mosqueda at Macmillan, our super talented designers Toni Tajima and Ralph Fowler, and Elinor Hutton, our project manager.

Index

About Tasting Table

Team Tasting Table eats and drinks around the globe, seeking out delicious discoveries to share with adventurous eaters everywhere. We proudly fill your feed with ideas that will inspire you to get out of your inbox and into the world, from restaurant recommendations to chefs' recipes to epicurean destinations and beyond.

We're an opinionated gang of always-curious, never-pretentious, order-one-of-everything-for-the-table taste obsessives.

We're the line cooks who invite you into the kitchen for a peek, the bartenders sliding you a drink just as your glass empties, and the always-hungry friends who will taste anything once.

We'll go any distance to find a great taste experience from high-end to low-brow, because snobs are boring and human shelf-life is short. Thirsty yet? Pull up a seat. Let's cook something together. Let's order another round. Let's live deliciously.

Join us as we tour the world of food and drink with the people who are shaping it at TastingTable.com and @TastingTable on the social networks that you haven't deleted yet.

About the Authors

About Geoff Bartakovics

Geoff founded Tasting Table in 2008 to create a website and newsletter for people who pursue eating and drinking like a sport. Since then he has grown the media brand to reach millions of foodies daily while entertaining literally thousands of friends (and plenty of strangers) at the kinds of parties on which *Cooking with Friends* is based. Geoff lives with his dog, Sukey Barksdale, in New York City, where he can easily feed his hunger for learning something new every day of the year.

About Todd Coleman

Todd Coleman has seen every side of the food world—behind the lens, on the page, and beyond. A graduate of the Culinary Institute of America, Coleman did not cling narrowly to one aspect of the field. Over the course of many sumptuous and creative years, he has been everything from executive food editor at *Saveur* and creative director at Tasting Table to producer at the Food Network and shooter-writer-editor for everything from travel stories to cookbooks. He cofounded the NYC-based creative agency Delicious Contents, and is currently the digital director of At-Sunrice GlobalChef Academy in Singapore and editor at large of Tasting Table.